The Perishers
OMN

By Maurice Dodd & Dennis Collins • Mirror Books

ORIGINAL CARTOON OFFER

A framed, original Perishers cartoon can be yours!

Due to the enormous popularity of The Perishers, we have decided to offer a selection of original cartoons by Maurice Dodd for just £65.00 each! Every cartoon comes to you framed and ready to hang on your wall. Just fill in the form below and post off your order today! We regret that it is impossible to supply specific cartoons of your choice.

ORDER FORM

Please send me:.......... original Perishers cartoons at £65.00 each. ________

Name ____________________

Address ____________________

____

____

Please make cheques payable to: Syndication International Ltd., and post to:

The Perishers original cartoon offer, Syndication International Ltd., 4/12 Dorrington Street, London EC1. Please allow 28 days for delivery.

1. *Of steadfast companionship and vanishing comestibles . . .*

Meet the stars of this cartoon collection, Wellington and Boot—a boy and his dog or, as the dog would have it, a dog and his boy.

Not that the dog cares much for his canine appellation since he considers himself to be not a dog but an eighteenth-century aristocrat (Captain Boot of O'Bunion's Intruders—a company of freebooters and freesockers and freemealers and anything else which was going) condemned to wear the mantle of a wall-to-wall rug through the curse of an unrequited Gipsy wench.

Side by side they go through life together, sharing whatever comes their way—provided neither of them can get to whatever it is first. A glance to the top of the page will show how steadfastly they look after each other—or rather at each other—to forestall whatever it is the other is planning on getting away with.

A glance to the lower right reveals Wellington, who's something of a philosopher, searching for the meaning of life—and his breakfast, which went missing at the very moment Boot chanced by.

Philosophy is not Boot's chosen subject. His tastes vary, depending on whatever is available to be tasted. At the moment portrayed, the subject he had chosen was breakfast.

2. *Of bamboo poles as an aid to romance . . .*

Meet two of the supporting cast (one of them—Marlon—has to be supported frequently, usually with a forked stick). Portrayed above, the wet looking object on the left is a boy, technically speaking, and the lumpy looking object on the right is a girl, though this definition strains the meaning of the word to its limit.

The boy answers to the name of Marlon—whenever he can remember that *is* his name. The girl goes by the name of Maisie. She also goes wherever Marlon goes. He is the consuming passion in her life, giving him the key to her heart and asking nothing in return save the precise location and value of the contents of his wallet.

Marlon doesn't return Maisie's fervour (in fact Marlon doesn't return anything since he's usually forgotten where he's put it, even minutes after he's borrowed it) but Maisie is undeterred and untiring in the pursuit of her desire. In the right-hand corner you can see her conducting a public opinion pole as to her desirability and popularity by playing 'he loves me—he loves me not' on Marlon's head. But she keeps ending with '. . . loves me not' which she regards as unacceptable and has to start all over again. It could be worse. She could be causing lasting damage by hitting him on his boots—which is where he keeps his brains.

3. *On infantile ingenuity, and there's no known cure for it . . .*

Meet the spanner in the works, the fly in the ointment, the spider in the bath, the toad in the hole (we speak here of a *real* toad) and glue on the loo. One Baby Grumpling, who is accredited with having invented all the aforementioned items.

Baby Grumpling, a kind of biological whoopee cushion, is Maisie's little brother, which accounts for Maisie's bad temper and assures that much will be forgiven her in the life to come, which, with a menace like Baby Grumpling at large, might be sooner than is normally anticipated.

It's not that there's evil in the infant's heart—he just has an enquiring mind. The kind of mind which, coming across a sleeping earhole, pokes a finger into the aperture just to see what the result might be. Such is Grumpling's propensity for annoyance, he even annoys himself, as can be witnessed by glancing top left. And in the right-hand corner below you can see how, tiring of the constant effort expended on getting Maisie into hot water, he is inviting her to do it for herself by plunging head first into the bucket he has so thoughtfully provided.

And now, gentle reader, follow Maisie's example and plunge into the book proper. You may not feel better when you emerge, but you'll certainly feel different.

HOWL
THANKS TO YOU OLE BOOT IS STUCK IN THE LAVATORY PAN — WHAT'RE YOU GOIN' T'DO ABOUT IT?
I'LL GO STRAIGHT HOME AN' SEE IF I C'N INVENT SUMTHIN' TO...
P.272
YOU'LL COME STRAIGHT IN HERE AN' DO A BIT OF PUSHIN' AN' PULLIN'
RIGHT— HEAVE
ARF ARF ARF ARF ARF
HE'S COMIN' — HE'S COMIN'
NOT THAT WAY— THIS WAY
HEAVE
WELL... AT LEAST YOU'LL BE ABLE TO SIT'N WATCH T.V.

SINCE I HAVEN'T YET THOUGHT OF A WAY TO GET YOU OUT OF THIS FIX, BOOT, I'VE COME HOME AT LUNCHTIME TO FEED YOU
P.273
BUT I HAVEN'T GOT MUCH TIME SO YOU'LL HAVE TO GET THIS DOWN IN A HURRY
LIKE A DRINKIES? HERE Y'ARE THEN — CRUMBS — IS THAT THE TIME?
— I'LL COME STRAIGHT HOME FROM SCHOOL — THE ONLY THING IS
WE MUS'N' LET THIS SORT OF TREATMENT SPOIL YOU

P.274
(HEY, PSST, MAISIE)
WELL ?
— HE STILL HAS TO HAVE SOME EXERCISE

P.275
I'VE THOUGHT OF A SOLOOSHUN TO BOOT'S PERDICAMENT
LET'S HOPE IT'S BETTER THAN YOUR PERNUNCIATION
Y'SEE THE PIPE IN THE BACK OF THE PAN ?
I DO INDEED
WELL IF WE PRODDED SOMETHIN' UP THERE WHAT'D MAKE 'IM JUMP
A 'OT POKER P'RAPS...
GRRRR
YOU'RE NOT AS IMMOBILISED AS YOU'VE LED ME TO BELIEVE, BOOT

I'VE THOUGHT OF A METHOD OF GETTIN' YOU OUT OF THAT THING, BOOT
IT'S CALLED A LIBERAL APPLICATION OF SEVERE FRIGHT
P.276

RIGHT, BOOT, WE'RE GOIN' TO PUSH THIS THING BACK WHERE IT BELONGS
TINKER
TINKER
PUSH
BONK
THAT SEEMS TO BE FIRMLY IN PLACE
WHILE I'M HERE I MIGHT AS WELL GIVE IT A TEST RUN
WELL — EVERYTHING SEEMS TO BE SATISFAC...
OH— OH
I FORGOT TO TAKE IT OFF THE SKATE BOARD
P.277

HULLO BOOT OLD FRUIT—ANY NEWS FOR THE NEWS-HOUND ?
I HAVEN'T BEEN IN A POSITION TO HEAR ANY NEWS
IN FACT I'VE BEEN IN A POSITION OF **CONSIDERABLE EMBARRASS-MENT**
P.278
OH ?
ARE IT SOMETHING SCANDALOUS CONCERNING A MEMBER OF THE OPPOSITE (SLURP) SEX ?
NO
A MEMBER OF THE (COUGH) SAME SEX ?
DAMME SIRRAH —**NO!**
OH WELL...
DRUGS ? CRIME ? PROSTITUTION ? MURDER ? SADISM ?
DON'T BE SILLY— I SPENT THE WEEK STUCK IN A LAVATORY PAN
GOODNESS GRACIOUSNESS — WE **CAN'T** PRINT A STORY LIKE **THAT**

WHY COULDN'T YOU PRINT MY STORY OF BEING STUCK IN THE LAVATORY PAN
NOT ENOUGH DRAMA —I WANT SOME HARD NEWS
WELL THE RIM WAS HARD ENOUGH I CAN TELL YOU
NOT ENOUGH HUMAN INTEREST
—UNLESS YOU COULD IMPLICATE SOME WELL-KNOWN PERSONALITY...
—PREFERABLY ONE WEARING A SLIT SKIRT SHOWING TANT-ALISING GLIMPSES OF FRILLY KNICKER
AND A BLOUSE WHICH SHOWS SIGNS OF BEING UNDER CONSIDERABLE STRAIN AT THE TOP END
P.279
—LISTEN B.H. — IF YOU'RE EXPECTING ME TO FABRICATE A STORY CONCERNING SOME WOMAN...
WOMAN? STOP, CEASE, DESIST— HAVE YOU NEVER HEARD OF THE **SEX EQUALITY** ACT

B.H. — ARE YOU TELLING ME YOU WANT A STORY CONCERNING A PERSON WEARING A SLIT SKIRT. BURSTING BLOUSE AND FRILLY DRAWERS
BUT YOU WON'T SPECIFY WHICH SEX ?
WE HAVE TO BE SO-O-O CAREFUL BOOT
— I DON'T MIND IF IT'S A MAN OR A WOMAN
— WITH BUMPS ON THE FRONT
P.280

B.H. (CALCUTTA) Failed
DO I UNDERSTAND YOU'RE SUGGESTING I EMBELLISH MY STORY OF BEING STUCK IN A LAVATORY PAN WITH FABRICATIONS ABOUT A SEXY WOMAN-TYPE PERSON ?
WHO, HOPEFULLY, HAS REVEALED SCANDALOUS DETAILS OF DRUG-CRAZED ORGIES IN THE LOCAL COUNCIL CHAMBERS . . .
AND EVEN FRUITIER GOINGS-ON BEHIND LOCKED DOORS
CERTAINLY NOT
(NOT WITHOUT OUR PAYING FOR IT)
P.281

SO NOW IT'S PAYMENT IS IT? — CHEQUE BOOK JOURNALISM
WELL ... NO REMEMBERING WE'RE SPEAKING OF THE 'WEST CRUNGE CLARION & DUBIOUS ADVERTISER'
IN OUR CASE IT ARE GREEN SHIELD STAMP JOURNALISM
P.282

SORRY B.H. (CALCUTTA) Failed — BUT I CAN'T INVENT NEWS STORIES — EVEN FOR YOUR SAKE
P.283
I MUST SAY I ...
DO YOU KNOW ...
... THAT'S THE FIFTH SNAIL THAT'S TRUNDLED PAST HERE THIS WEEK, I WONDER ...
AHA!
RESIDENTS' FURY OVER HIGH ST. TRAFFIC — SAY ON — SAY ON

RAGING AT THE INCREASE (NO—DANGEROUS INCREASE) IN HIGH ST. TRAFFIC RESIDENTS ROUNDED IN FURY ON...
WHAT'RE YOU DOING B.H.?
A?
I'M MAKING NOTES
ON MY NOTE-PAD
I MEAN WHAT'S ALL THIS DANGEROUS TRAFFIC AND RESIDENTS' FURY TARRA-DIDDLE
OVER SNAILS?
ISN'T IT A BIT LUDICROUS?
MMM —MAYBE YOU'RE RIGHT, BOOT
"CURTAIL ELEPHANT MENACE" LOCAL'S DEMAND
P.284

ELEPHANT MENACE TO LIFE AND PROPERTY FURORE (BUT GARDENERS EXPECT PILES OF BENEFITS)
DAMME SIRRAH—THIS IS NONSENSICAL
I STARTED OFF TALKING OF FIVE SNAILS AND YOU'VE ENLARGED THAT TO MENACING ELEPHANTS POUNDING THROUGH THE HIGH ST.
WELL I'VE HAD ENOUGH—AT THE RATE YOU'RE GOING ON
RATE REVOLT THREATENED
P.285

A HARASSED COUNCIL FACED WITH A PLAGUE OF ELEPHANTS IN THE HIGH STREET WAS TODAY REELING UNDER THE ADDED THREAT OF A RATE REVOLT..
BY THE LORD HARRY, B.H., I'LL LEAVE YOU TO YOUR RAVINGS
SNIFF SNIFF
— I'VE BETTER THINGS TO DO
(I'M SURE IT WAS HEREABOUTS MUTTER MUTTER)
WHAT'RE YOU DOING BOOT ?
LOOKING FOR A BONE I BURIED THE OTHER NIGHT
I'M SURE IT WAS ROUND HERE
P.286
NAKED BONE MIDNIGHT BURIAL DRAMA (WHAT IS THE GRIM SECRET OF THE LOST TOMB)

'MIDNIGHT NAKED BONE BURIAL — RUMOURS OF SATANIC ORGIES WERE RIFE...
P.287
AS OUR REPORTER (NO MAKE THAT OUR GALLANT REPORTER) RISKED LIFE AND...
STUFF!
STUFF ?
STUFF AND NONSENSE SIRRAH — RARELY HAVE I HEARD SUCH A FARRAGO OF FATUITY
WELL YOU'LL GET NO MORE FROM ME — I'LL NOT BREATHE ANOTHER WORD — MY LIPS ARE SEALED
PERILS OF MISUSING SUPER-GLUE — CORONER'S WARNING
MMMMM

WELL SINCE I'VE EXHAUSTED YOUR MEAGRE FUND OF NEWS I'LL HAVE TO TURN MY ATTENTIONS ELSEWHERE
—IT'S BACK TO BRICKS WITHOUT STRAW—BUILDING ON SHAKY FOUNDATIONS
YOU MEAN INVENTING MORE NEWS BY EXAGGERATING ORDINARY EVERY-DAY EVENTS ?
OH NO—I'M NOT TALKING ABOUT MY ORDINARY JOB AS A JOURNALIST
I REFER TO MY SECONDARY PRESTIGIOUS CAREER
AS A PUBLIC RELATIONS DOG TO 'BABEL CONSTRUCTIONS'
A GROUP OF EXTREMELY INEFFICIENT BUILDING CONTRACTORS
SITE OFFI CE
P.288

MIRROR MIRROR ON THE WALL— WHO IS THE FAIREST OF THEM ALL
THOU MAISIE ART FAIREST IN THE LAND
(WHICH AIN'T TOO HARD TO UNDERSTAND)
if thy judgement matched thy voice methinks thee'd made a different choice
P.289

P.290
maisie— what do worms do in the winter?
A?
What do the poor little worms do when the ground is cold and hard?
OH... WELL... I SHOULDN'T WORRY, BABY GRUMPLIN'
THOSE WORMIKINS ARE SNUG AN' COSY WITH THEIR WORM MUMMIES AND DADDIES AN' WORM HOT WATER BOTTLES AN' PROBABLY LOVELY HOT CUPS OF WARM OVALTINE
you know maisie—there are those who consider you brash, unfeelin' an' insensitive
OH YES
but some could think of you as sensitive, imaginative and kind
OH... YES?
personally—i'm of the opinion you're just half-baked

you know maisie — one of the things you said wasn't quite as silly as it sounded
— about worms having drinks of ovaltine
— they must fancy a hot drink as much as anybody
mind you — they haven't half got a thirst
— that's about five gallons i've poured down there this morning
P.291

YOU'RE POURIN' PERFECTLY GOOD OVALTINE DOWN THERE FOR THE WORMS ?
P.292
GIMME THAT!
well it's not *just* ovaltine maisie — it's more what you'd call wormvaltine
it contains added nourishment
— it's got beetles in it

P.293
here you are then — nice and hot — do you the world of good
and now — after me — one - two - three...
we are the wormvaltinies...

OH YES
YOU MANAGED TO TALK MUM INTO FEELIN' SORRY FOR THE WORMS
SO'S YOU COULD GO ON GIVIN' 'EM THAT ROTTEN WORMVALTINE STUFF
OH YES YOU'RE GOOD AT THAT (SNIFF) — GETTIN' ROUN' MUM
i'm even better at it than you think
this happens to be molevaltine
P.294

SIGH
WHAT IS IT THIS TIME ?
WORMVALTINE OR MOLEVALTINE ?
horsevaltine
P.295

YOU CAN'T GO ROUN' GIVIN' OVALTINE TO THE WHOLE ANIMAL KINGDOM
WHO D'YOU THINK YOU ARE— St.FRANCIS ?
AN' EVEN **HE** DIN'T GO ABOUT DISHIN' OUT FREE OVALTINE
well— perhaps **his** mummy wouldn't **give** him any
P.296

NOW you're all right then
a ?
oh you'll soon feel the benefit...
NOW WHAT ?
i jus' saved these worms from certain 'stinction
i found them frozen stiff
—and popped them in front of the fire for a bit of a warm
LISTEN— WORMS AREN'T **SUPPOSED** TO BE POPPED IN FRONT OF A FIRE—THEY DON'T **NEED** A BIT OF A WARM
YOU KNOW WHAT YOU'VE GOT THERE NOW ? TWO **NICELY GRILLED** WORMS
oh well
NOW WHAT'RE YOU FERRETIN' ABOUT FOR ?
—a couple of slices of bread
P.297

it can't be very good out in that cold damp garden
much more snug and warm in here
BABY GRUMPLIN' — IF YOU'VE BROUGHT ANOTHER WORM INTO THIS HOUSE . . .
no maisie — i haven't, honest, cross mi heart
JUST AS WELL
how d'you feel about hedgehogs ?
P.298

A HEDGEHOG ?
IN THE HOUSE ?
CRIPES WHAT A VOICE
ARE YOU MAD ?
THINK OF THE FLEAS
I THINK I'LL TAKE MY CHANCE ON THE MOTORWAY
don't worry maisie — i have
mind you — i had a terrible job getting them off that hedgehog
P.299

WORMS — HEDGEHOGS AN' NOW FLEAS IN THE HOUSE
WELL I'M GOIN' TO BLOW THE GAFF — I'M TELLIN' MUM
if you do, maisie i'll tell mum what you did
CRIPES —WOTTA VOICE
JUMP FOR IT BOYS
GERMOLINO
P.300
YOU'RE BLUFFIN' BABY GRUMPLIN' — YOU DON'T KNOW I DID ANYTHIN' —YOU'VE GOT NOTHIN' ON ME
i'll tell mum to watch your face when i tell mum you've obviously done something
WE'LL TAKE OUR CHANCES WITH THE PEST CONTROL DEPT.
and what's more...
...once i saw her face change i knew it was worth while pushing on for a packet of smarties

MUM — ARE THERE ANY CHRIS'MAS PREZZIES HIDDEN IN THE HOUSE ?
NO MAISIE
P.301
MUM — ARE YOU SURE THERE AREN'T ANY CHRIS'MAS PREZZIES HIDDEN IN THE HOUSE ?
YES MAISIE
I PROMISE I WON'T GO LOOKIN FOR THEM IF YOU TELL ME THERE ARE CHRIS'MAS PREZZIES HIDDEN IN THE HOUSE
MAISIE — THERE ARE NO CHRISTMAS PRESENTS HIDDEN IN THE HOUSE
CRUMBS MUM — ARE YOU TELLIN' ME I'M GOIN' TO HAVE TO LOOK BACK ON AN UNHAPPY CHILDHOOD

CRUMBS MUM — IT'S NOT GOIN' TO BE MUCH OF A CHRIS'MAS IS IT MUM ?
P.302
NOT IF THERE AREN'T ANY CHRIS'MAS PARCELS AN'...
MAISIE — I HOPE YOU'RE NOT BEING A GREEDY LITTLE GIRL
TRUE HAPPINESS DOES NOT COME WRAPPED IN CHRISTMAS PARCELS
BUT MUM — I DON'T WANT YOU WORRYIN' OVER MY HAPPINESS MUM
I'M PREPARED TO MAKE DO WITH THE SHORT-TERM ILLUSION OF PLEASURE — SUCH AS WOT YOU GET IN A CHRIS'MAS PARCEL

AH-HA !
P.303
WHAT'RE YOU DOIN' IN THAT CUPBOARD MARLON ?
I'LL BET YOU'RE HIDIN' A CHRIS'MAS PARCEL
LEAVE IT OUT MAISIE — THERE'S NO PARCEL OR ANYTHIN' ELSE IN THIS CUPBOARD WOT CONCERNS YOU
I'LL BET YOU'RE HIDIN' MY PREZZY IN THERE — GET OUTA THE WAY
HOW DESPICABLE — YOU WERE TELLIN' THE TRUTH

I BET THERE'S CHRIS'MAS PARCELS HIDDEN SOMEWHERE HERE — I JUS' BET
CRUMBS MAISIE — LEAVE ORF, DO
THERE'S **NO** PARCELS — **NOTHIN'** IF YOU DON'T BELIEVE ME, GO AHEAD AN' **SEARCH**
SOME PARCELS ARE LONG AN' THIN AN' COULD BE HIDDEN UP A PERSON'S TROUSER LEG
P.304

'TWAS THE NIGHT BEFORE CHRIS'MAS AN' ALL THROUGH THE HOUSE NO CREATURE WAS STIRRIN' NOT EVEN A MOUSE ...
as a matter of fact you're wrong there
there are several rampaging behind the skirting board
as well as silver-fish skating round the bathroom, a beetle boozing in the larder, a cockroach muttering behind the washing machine and a dirty great spider grunting and stamping under your bed
i record these facts in the interest of veracity — g'night
P.305

IT'S THE MESSAGE OF CHRIS'MAS WHICH COUNTS, BOOT, NOT ALL THE OTHER TRAPPIN'S
P.306
I MEAN — WE MAY NOT HAVE MUCH AN' WE DI'N GET MUCH BUT THE MESSAGE OF CHRIS'MAS IS ONE OF HOPE
HOPE — HOPE FOR US ALL — HOPE FOR THE YEAR TO COME
— AN' NEX' YEAR I HOPE I'LL GET A MOTORBIKE AN' A REAL COWBOY GUN AN' A BIG CAKE AN'...

WHAT DID YOU GET FOR CHRIS'MAS, BABY GRUMPLIN' ?
very little
— owing to industrial action in santa's workshop
or because of falling production and redundancies caused by the misplaced credit squeeze on fairy gold
accounts differ, from various adult sources
my own observations indicate that none of these problems affected production at santa's brewery
P.307

WHAT SORT OF A CHRIS'MAS DID YOU HAVE MARLON ?
OH—WE 'AD A REAL FAMBLY CHRIS'MAS
WERE ALL THE FAMILY THERE ?
YEA—MINE YOU, DAD DIN'T WANT TO ASK AUNT ETHEL'S LOT
BUT MUM SAID "FORGIVE AN' FORGET" SO WE EVEN 'AD AUNT ETHEL'S LOT
WE'RE PUTTIN' THE GLASS BACK IN NEX' WEEK
P.308

WHAT SORT OF A CHRIS'MAS DID YOU HAVE, MAISIE ?
NOT BAD —BUT THAT RATBAG MARLON DIN'T EVEN BUY ME A PREZZY
BUT HE *SAID* HE WASN' GOIN' TO BUY YOU A PREZZY
I KNOW— THAT'S TYPICAL OF MARLON THAT IS
Y'CAN'T EVEN TRUST HIM TO BREAK HIS WORD
P.309

WHAT'RE YOU DOIN' MARLON — REVISIN' YOUR NEW YEAR RESOLUTION ?
Q.1
DON' BE FEEBLE WELLIN'TON — I'M WORKIN' ON MY NEW PROJECT — RAISIN' THE LUCY-TAINIER
YOU'RE GOIN' TO RAISE THE LUSITANIA ?
NOT JUS' ME — NOT ON MY OWN D'YOU THINK I'M STUPID ?
THA'S A'RIGHT THEN
W-E-L-L ... NO
I'M JUS' MAKIN' A LIST OF MY REQUIREMENDS
ITEM : ONE DIVER
MAY I RECONSIDER MY ANSWER TO YOUR LAST QUESTION ?

YOU'VE REALLY COMMITTED YOUR TOTAL THINKIN' INPUT TO THIS ONE, HAVEN'T YOU MARLON ?
I MEAN — RAISIN' THE LUSITANIA...
WITH ONE DIVER
WELL WOT ELSE WELLIN'TON ? THERE'S NOT MUCH POINT IN A FOOTBALLER OR A PIANIST — IT'S GOT T'BE A DIVER — ATTENTION TO DETAIL LIKE THAT'S IMPORTANT
AH, THOUGH — WAIT A MO...
I THINK I'M GOIN' TO BE SORRY I ASKED — BUT WHY ONE IRISH DIVER ?
— ONE IRISH DIVER
Q.2
'COS I HAPPEN TO KNOW THE LUCY TAINIER'S SUNK IN THE IRISH SEA
REGRET SWEEPS O'ER ME LIKE A CLOUD

RAISING THE LUCY-TAINIER FROM THE SEA-BED
(A SERIES OF STUDIES AND PROJECTS BY MARLON)
PROJECT 1
Q.3
You will need ......
① A VERY LONG POLE
② SUMBODY WHO'S GOOD AT PULLING (BEST GET SUMBODY BIGGER AND STRONGER THAN YOURSELF. KING KONG WOOD BE IDEEL)
IDEEL
③ A BIT OF IRELAND
D
A
B
C
SEA BED
Method:
STAND ON YOUR PORTION OF IRELAND Ⓐ PLACE POLE Ⓑ UNDER LUCY TAINIER Ⓒ AND PULL DOWN LIKE MAD (WHY IT'S BEST TO GET SUMBODY ELSE TO DO THIS IS BECAUSE THE BOAT MAY COME UNSTUCK ALL OF A SUDDEN AND SHOOT UP IN THE AIR AND THE PULLER Ⓓ WILL FALL FLAT ON HIS BACK)

YOU DON'T SPELL *LUSITANIA* LIKE THAT
LIKE WOT?
LUCY-TAINIER
Q.4
LIKE **THAT** IT'S NOT T-A-I-N-I-E-R — IT'S T-A-N-I-A
OH YES?
LUCY-TAINIER
— I WAS READIN' THE OTHER DAY — ABOUT THIS BLOKE — PRINCE R-A-N-I-A....
LUCY-TAINIER

RAISING THE LUCY-TAINIER FROM THE SEA-BED
(A SERIES OF STUDIES AND PROJECTS BY MARLON)
PROJECT 2
Q.5
you will need......
① LOTS OF PEESES OF STRONG STRING
3 DOZEN NEW LAID PLEES
CRIPES!
② LOTS OF ANT'S EGGS
③ LOTS AND LOTS OF STRONG FISHES (WALES WOOD BE IDEEL)
IDEEL
Method Ⓐ
~~ATTASH~~ ~~ATTATCH~~ TIE FISHES TO LUCY TAINIER WITH PEESES OF STRING
Ⓑ DISTRIBUTE GENEROUS PORSHUN OF ANTS EGGS ON SURFACE OF SEA
Note: SELECT ONLY FISHES WITH VERY STRONG TAILS

RAISING THE LUCY-TAINIER FROM THE SEA-BED
(A SERIES OF STUDIES AND PROJECTS BY MARLON)
PROJECT 3
Q.6
you will need...
① LOTS OF BITS OF HOSES
② LOTS OF PUMPS
③ LOTS OF FRENDS (FOR THIS PROJECT, CASHWELL ACWAINTENSES WILL DO)
Method: ① ATTATCH FRENDS TO ENDS OF PUMPS. ATTATCH HOSES TO OTHER ENDS OF PUMPS. ATTATCH OTHER ENDS OF HOSES TO SHIP (IT'S IMPORTANT TO GET THIS RITE OR FRENDS WILL BE PUMPING UP EACH OTHER'S PUMPS-OR WORSE.) ② PUMP LIKE MAD
RITE ✓
RONG ✗
EVEN RONGER ✗✗
THE PUMPED-IN AIR WILL RAISE THE SHIP TO THE SURFACE
Note: AT THIS POINT IT'S ADVISABEL TO STOP PUMPING

ER... MARLON...
THAT LAST IDEA OF YOURS FOR RAISIN' THE LUSITANIA, BY PUMPIN' IT FULL OF AIR...
COULD YOU HAVE POSSIBLY MISSED A POINT?
I MEAN — THE LUSITANIA'S FULL OF HOLES
...PORTHOLES... FUNNELS — TO SAY NOTHIN' OF THE HOLES MADE BY TORPEDOES
I KNOW OTHERWISE I COULDN'T PUMP THE AIR IN
BUT LEAKS MARLON, LEAKS DON'T YOU THINK YOU SHOULD TELL PEOPLE HOW TO TAKE CARE OF LEAKS
OH VERY WELL WELLIN'TON — IF YOU SAY SO
TAKING CARE OF LEEKS
① LEEKS NEED LOTS OF WATER
THOUGH IT ALL SEEMS A BIT IRREVERENT TO ME
THANKS BOYO
② IN THE WINTER LITTLE NITTED LEEK-BONNETS ARE MUCH APREESHEEATED
Q.7

SLAM
'LO WELLIN'TON YOU LOOK A BIT...
FRAUGHT? IS THAT THE WORD?
RATTLED? BOTHERED? BOGGLED? BUT MOST OF ALL MARLON'D?
HE'S IN THERE PLANNIN' TO RAISE THE LUSITANIA!
BY PUMPIN' IT FULL OF AIR
AN' WHEN I ASK HIM 'WHAT ABOUT THE LEAKS?' — KNOW WHAT HE DOES?
— HE STARTS DRAWIN' LITTLE WOOLLY HATS
WOOLLY HATS FOR LEEKS
END WHAT, PRECASELY, MAKES YOU THINK YOU KNOW MORE ABOUT GROWIN LEEKS THEN MAY MAWLON?
Q.8

♫ YOO-HOO MARLON — YOO-HOO KISSY-FACE ?
WELLIN'TON TELLS ME YOU'RE WORKIN' ON PLANS TO RAISE THE LUSITANIA
THA'S RIGHT — I'M NOW ON PROJECT Nº 4
OOH — AN' TO THINK I USED TO THINK YOU HAD NO AMBITION
WHAT'RE THOSE YOU'RE DRAWIN' ?
— CORKS
CORKS ?
ER... MARLON... THE LUSITANIA'S ***VERY HEAVY***
OH ALL RIGHT THEN — ***'LOTS*** OF CORKS'
BUT MARLON — IT ***REALLY IS*** VERY VERY VERY ***VERY*** HEAVY
— 'LOTS'N LOTS'N LOTS'N ***LOTS*** OF CORKS'
BUT MARLON...
I 'OPE YOU'RE NOT GOIN' TO START ***NIT-PICKIN'***
Q.9

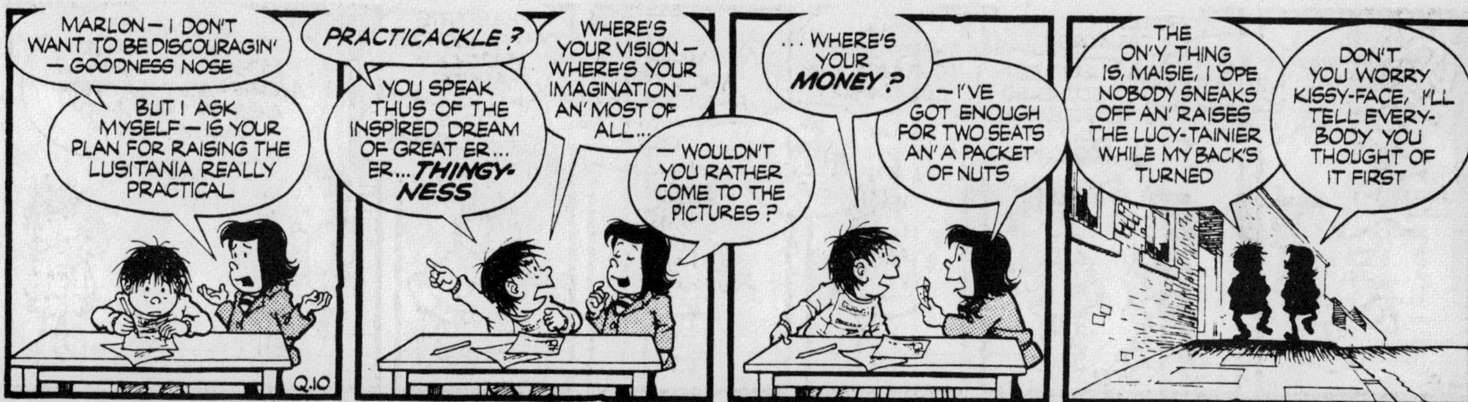
MARLON — I DON'T WANT TO BE DISCOURAGIN' — GOODNESS NOSE
BUT I ASK MYSELF — IS YOUR PLAN FOR RAISING THE LUSITANIA REALLY PRACTICAL
Q.10
PRACTICACKLE ?
YOU SPEAK THUS OF THE INSPIRED DREAM OF GREAT ER... ER... ***THINGY-NESS***
WHERE'S YOUR VISION — WHERE'S YOUR IMAGINATION — AN' MOST OF ALL...
— WOULDN'T YOU RATHER COME TO THE PICTURES ?
... WHERE'S YOUR ***MONEY ?***
— I'VE GOT ENOUGH FOR TWO SEATS AN' A PACKET OF NUTS
THE ON'Y THING IS, MAISIE, I 'OPE NOBODY SNEAKS OFF AN' RAISES THE LUCY-TAINIER WHILE MY BACK'S TURNED
DON'T YOU WORRY KISSY-FACE, I'LL TELL EVERY-BODY YOU THOUGHT OF IT FIRST

MIRROR MIRROR ON THE WALL — WHO IS THE FAIREST OF THEM ALL ?
Q.11
YOU ARE MAISIE — THAT'S WHO, YOU'RE A KNOCKOUT, MAGIC, GOR-GEOUS — OH THE MEN ARE PUTTY IN YOUR HAN'S
♪ LOVELY TO LOOK AT DELIGHTFUL TO HOLD AN' HEAVEN TO KISS.... ♪
THIS MIRROR'S BEEN DRINKIN'

MARLON — DO YOU THINK I'M BEAUTIFUL ?
A ?
Q.12
OR P'RAPS YOU'D PREFER... PRETTY ?
ER...
OR POSSIBLY — ATTRACTIVE ?
UMM...
APPEALIN' ?
NICE LOOKIN' ?
MMFFF
LISTEN BOY— IF YOU DON'T SPEAK UP BEFORE WE GET DOWN TO "BASEMENT — AN' KITCHEN SINKS" YOU'RE GOIN' TO BE IN TROUBLE

A WOMAN KNOWS INSTINCTIVELY WHEN SHE'S LOSIN' HER MAN...
Q.13
AN' SEEKS REMEDY IN THE PRIMAL DEPTHS OF THE FEMININE SOUL
DRAWIN' FROM THE FATHOMLESS MYSTERY THE DARK COILIN' SECRETS OF SUCH AS HELEN-OF-TROY, CLEOPATRA, MATA HARI, MAGGIE SHELTON...
CREATIN' BY SUBTLE ALCHEMY A NET TO ENSLAVE THE WAYWARD MALE
LAST GASP
—THIS SHOULD WORK A TREAT

IF THIS STUFF WORKS ON FLIES IT SHOULD WORK A TREAT ON MARLON
Q.14
BUT P'RAPS I SHOULD TEST IT ON AT LEAST ONE HUMAN BEAN
AFTER ALL—I DON'T WANT TO DAMAGE MY PROSPECT
OH WELL-IN'-TON
WOULD YOU MIND TAKIN' PART IN AN EXPERIMENT?
ARE YOU EXPERIENCIN' AN UNCONTROLLABLE URGE TO RAIN 'OT BURNIN' KISSES ON THE UPTURNED PETAL OF MY FACE?

WELL, MY POTENT PONG PERSUADER CERTAINLY WORKED ON WELLIN'TON
OOOGH
Q.15
BUT WELLIN'TON IS NOT THE MAN I WANT
ON THE OTHER HAND— AS FAR AS THE EYE CAN SEE
HE'S THE ONLY MAN THERE ***IS***
GAH
AN' ***WHERE*** D'YOU THINK ***YOU'RE*** GOIN', BUSTER ?

RIGHT, BOYO—YOU'RE ABOUT TO GET YOURSELF LOVED TO THE LIMITS
COR —LOOK AT HIM— PUTTY IN MY HANDS
Q.16
BUT WAIT— IS ***THIS*** WHAT I ***WANT***— A MERE ***PUPPET*** READY TO DO MY EVERY BIDDIN' ?
JUST A ***PLAYTHING*** WITH NO WILL OF ITS OWN ?
LISTEN, MAISIE . . .
YOU SPEAK WHEN YOU'RE SPOKEN TO

RIGHT— C'MERE YOU GORGEOUS (AN' WHAT'S MORE ONLY ONE AVAILABLE) HUNK YOU
GET READY FOR A RATION OF PASSION YOU LUCKY BOY
SQUIRP SQUIRP
MIND YOU — YOU'RE ONLY A SUBSTITUTE
YOU WOULDN' BE GETTIN' THIS A-TALL IF MARLON WAS AROUN'
SQUIRP SQUIRP SQUIRP
YEUK YEUK YEUK
SOME PEOPLE ARE BORN LUCKY
Q.17

C'MERE WELLIN'TON— YOU ACTION-PACKED SEX-POT YOU
SQUIRP SQUIRP
YEUK
THIS'LL KEEP ME IN TRAININ' TILL . . .
. . . MARLON !
MARLON — WHAT'RE YOU DOIN' UNDER THERE ?
THERE ISN'T ANY-BODY UNDER HERE
AN' IF THERE IS — IT'S THE GAS-MAN
— READIN' THE METER
WELL, GASMAN, THAT METER HAPPENS TO BE A BUGGY
SOMEBODY AT HEAD OFFICE IS GOIN' TO HEAR ABOUT THIS
Q.18

STILL GOIN' TO PRETEND YOU'RE A GASMAN, MARLON ?
♫ 'TWAS A JOLLY GASMAN WHO GOT OUT HIS METER-PAD
WELL PERHAPS A DOSE OF MY POTENT PONG PERSUADER WILL CURE THAT
UNDER THE SHADE OF A... ♪
RIGHT 'GASMAN' — WHAT'VE YOU GOT TO SAY TO *THAT* ?
NO MAISIE, *NO*
CLEAR THE AREA — EXTINGUISH ALL NAKED FLAMES !
Q.19

RIGHT, MARLON — TAKE THAT AN' THAT AN' *THAT*
STOP THAT, MAISIE
I THINK YOU'RE GOIN' TO FIND ME IRRESISTABABBLE
HE'S MY *BEST FRIEN'* — I *WON'T* LET YOU *DO* THAT TO MY *BEST FRIEN'*
STAN' BACK — *STAN' BACK*
ONE MORE STEP AN' YOU'LL GET *ANOTHER* DOSE *YOURSELF*
REDUCIN' YOU ONCE AGAIN TO A MERE *PUPPET* — A *PLAYTHING* FOR MY DESIRES
GAH
WHERE WOULD YOU LIKE HIM DELIVERED ?
Q.20

COME ON MARLON — WALKIES
GAH
A BIT OF EXERCISE WILL TONE YOU UP — I'M SURE TO FEEL THE BENEFIT
WHAT'S GOIN' ON MAISIE ?
OH — 'LO PLAIN JANE
URGLE
THIS IS THE NEW MALLEABLE MARLON
UNDER THE INFLUENCE OF MY POTENT PONG PERSUADER
OH — I WISH HE WERE MINE
YOURS ?
A PRIME PROPERTY LIKE THIS ?
I MEAN... HONESTLY... WHAT COULD YOU POSSIBLY HAVE TO OFFER...
ONLY HALF AN HOUR, MIND YOU
UNLESS YOU'VE GOT TWO MARS BARS
Q.21

I'LL JUST GIVE HIM ANOTHER SPRAY — TO MAKE SURE HE'S NOT IN HIS RIGHT MIND
RIGHT — GOT Y'R CHOC'LATE BAR ?
HALF'N HOUR ONLY, MIND YOU
AN' YOU HAVE TO PAY FOR BREAKAGES
DON'T YOU THINK YOU MIGHT BE OVERDOIN' THIS ?
Q.22

CHEW CHEW LICK GOBBLE CHEW BITE CHEW
COME IN NUMBER 25
YOUR TIME IS UP
MMMM
SQUIRP
SQUIRP
SQUIRP
SLOBBER
Q.23

MAKE THE MOMENT LAST
WITH FRY'S (LICK SUCK CHEW SLOBBER GOBBLE) CHOC'LATE CREAM
MY TURN —I'VE PAID MY CHOC'LATE BAR
GERROFF —I'VE PAID TWO
OOH — LET ME AT 'IM
YUMMY
SQUIRP
SQUIRP
SQUIRP
GAH
SQUIRP
DREAM-BOAT
MIND YOUR... AAGH
LOOKIT ME — I'M SWOONIN'— I'M SWOONIN'
Q.24

I'M WITHDRAWIN' YOU FOR A BIT OF REST AN' RECUPERATION MARLON
'COS WE DON'T WANT YOU WORN OUT BEFORE YOUR TIME
WITH CARE YOU COULD LAST AT LEAST ANOTHER WEEK
ANYWAY I'VE DRIED UP THE SUPPLY OF CHOC'LATE BARS FOR THE TIME BEING
Q.25
AHA!
THE DAY OF RECKONIN' HAS ARRIVED
YOU'RE ABOUT TO TASTE YOUR OWN MEDICINE MAISIE
TAKE THAT
WHERE AM I ? WHAT HAPPENED ?
GOODNESS GRACIOUS — WHAT'S HAPPENED TO ME ?
I FIND I'M NO LONGER ABLE TO RESIST THE ADVANCES OF MEN
EASY PREY TO EVEN THEIR (TEE-HEE) DARKEST DESIRES
I'M YOURS — I'M YOURS
SQUIRP SQUIRP
'ULLO — IT'S MY OLE FRIEN' WELLIN'TON
JUS' CALL ME FRANKENSTEIN

UNDER THE INFLUENCE OF THE POTENT PONG PERSUADER, I AM NO LONGER IN CONTROL OF MYSELF
I'M YOURS MARLON — TO DO WITH AS YOU WILL (I HOPE)
YEUK
ALL RIGHT THEN
— WELLIN'TON — I'M YOURS
LIKEWISE YEUK
Q.26
WELL — SOMEBODY — MAKE ME AN OFFER!

Y'KNOW, BOOT, THE OLE PLACE IS LOOKIN' VERY TATTY
IT NEEDS A GOOD CLEAN UP
AN' YOU YOURSELF COULD DO WITH A...
BATH
AN' IT'S NO USE YOU TRYIN' TO HIDE
ONCE I'VE DECIDED ON A CLEAN-UP THERE'S GOIN' TO *BE* A CLEAN-UP
MIND YOU — I HADN'T DECIDED TO DO UNDER THE BEDS YET — BUT IT'S A START
Q.27

WHAT A RIGHT MESS YOU'RE IN NOW, BOOT — WITH BED-FLUFF ALL OVER YOU
I'LL GO AN' GET THE VACUUM CLEANER
WITH ANY LUCK WE MIGHT GET SOME OF THE ORIGINAL DIRT OFF AS WELL
AN' WHAT FOOL PUT THE REVERSE SWITCH ON?
Q.28

NOW LOOK AT THE STATE OF YOU
Q.29
NOW YOU'RE DEFINITELY GOIN' T'GET A BATH
YOU'RE ONLY DELAYIN' THE INEVITABLE YOU KNOW

WELL BOOT— YOU BEIN' COVERED WITH BED-FLUFF...
Q.30
PLUS BEIN' BLOWN OVER WITH THE CONTENTS OF THE VACUUM CLEANER...
ON TOP OF YOUR ORIGINAL DIRT...
ALL ADDS UP TO B-A-T-H BATH
BOOT ?
WHERE ARE YOU BOOT ?
YOU'RE NOT IMPROVIN' YOUR CHANCES BY HIDIN' IN THE COAL-HOLE

BED-FLUFF, THE CONTENTS OF THE VACUUM CLEANER AND NOW COAL
D'YOU THINK YOU COULD MANAGE TO COVER YOURSELF WITH ANYTHIN' ELSE ?
THAT WAS NOT MEANT AS A CHALLENGE YOU HAIRY GREAT CLOWN
Q.31

NOW LOOK AT YOU — ALL COVERED WITH FEATHERS
WHILE YOU'RE AT IT WHY DON'T YOU TRY TO FLY ?
NEVER MIND NEVER MIND!
Q.32

BOOT ? WHERE ARE YOU, BOOT ?
YOUR BATH IS READY
COME ON, BOOT
A BATH FULL OF LOVELY HOT WATER
HOT WATER ? NOW THERE'S A NOVELTY
WHEN DID THEY DISCONTINUE THE USE OF MOLTEN LEAD
Q.33

BOOT—ARE YOU GOIN' TO HAVE THIS BATH OR NOT ?
Q.34
NOT
LISTEN RUG-FACE — I WASN' GIVIN' YOU A CHOICE— THAT WAS WHAT'S KNOWN AS A RHETORICAL QUESTION
AND THIS IS WHAT'S KNOWN AS A RHETORICAL REFUSAL

YOU'RE NOT GETTIN' AWAY FROM ME I C'N TELL YOU
Q.35
THE NAME WELLIN'TON IS A BYWORD FOR DETERMINATION, TENACITY AN'... AN'...
— SAME-DAY SPEED-E FURNITURE REMOVAL ?

YOU WON'T GET AWAY FROM ME, BOOT — YOU WON'T — YOU *WON'T*
Q.36
OLE IRON-GRIP WELLIN'TON IS WHAT THEY CALL ME
WELL BY THE TIME THIS IS OVER YOU MAY HAVE ACQUIRED A FEW EXTRA TITLES

WHAT'S THIS COMING UP THE ROAD ?
IT... IT'S WELLINGTON
HM... YES
— DRAWIN' ATTENTION TO HIMSELF AS USUAL
Q.37

ALL RIGHT — ALL RIGHT
GO YOUR WAY — I GIVE IN
BUT I WANT YOU TO KNOW YOUR CONDUCT HAS BEEN DISGRACEFUL
AN' WHILE I MAY HAVE LOST THE ARGUMENT, I FEEL THAT I AT LEAST EMERGE WITH A CERTAIN DIGNITY
I TRUST I MAKE MYSELF CLEAR
CLEAR ENOUGH FOR THE AVERAGE REFUSE BAG, I'D SAY
Q.38

— OOH LOOK
. . . AN' LOOK AT THE STATE YOU'VE GOT ME IN — I MUST'VE GATHERED HALF THE RUBBISH . . .
Q.39
A MOBILE HOME
. . . IN THE DISTRICT
GET OFF — GET OFF
'FRAID IT'S NOT SUITABLE — YOUR DAD COULDN'T HAVE STOOD THE NOISE

CRUMBS I'LL NEVER GET RID OF ALL THIS MUCK AN' RUBBISH
IT'S ME WHO NEEDS A BATH NOW — THANKS TO YOU
Q.40
H'LO WELLIN'TON
YEA — WE SAW YOU SHOWIN' OFF AN'. . . CRUMBS WHAT'S THAT SMELL ?
SMELL ?
DOWN BOOT — DOWN BOY
TEE - HEE

ON TOP OF EVERYTHING I'M NOW TOLD I SMELL
I DON'T BELIEVE I SMELL ALL THAT BADLY
SNIFF
SNIFF
Q.41
—'LO DIRTY McSQUIRTY
—'LO WELLIN'TON
IF THERE'S ONE THING I CAN'T STAND IT'S SARCASTIC FLIES

THIS ALL STARTED OUT WITH YOU SUPPOSED TO BE HAVIN' A BATH
Q.42
AN' IT ENDS UP WITH ME HAVIN' TO HAVE A BATH
I S'POSE YOU FIND IT ALL HIGHLY...
...AMUSIN'
—I CANNOT TELL A LIE...

ALL RIGHT ALL RIGHT YOU STUPID DOG
HERE'S ANOTHER MESS YOU'VE LANDED ME IN
AN' IT'S NOT FUNNY— LET ME TELL YOU I DON'T THINK ANY OF THIS IS FUNNY
PITY THAT
— WE'VE GOT A REALLY CHEERY CHORTLE COMING UP
Q.43

WELL THAT'S IT—THE LAST STRAW—THE FINAL DEGRIMATION
ALL BECAUSE YOU WOULDN'T HAVE A BATH
I DON'T KNOW WHY I BOTHER WITH YOU
YOU BOTHER WITH ME BECAUSE I'M GREAT BIG LOVABLE OLD BOOT—THAT'S WHY
YOU'RE NOTHIN' BUT A GREAT AWKWARD MESSY STUPID OLE RUG-FACED LUMP
—LOVABLE YOU FORGOT LOVABLE
LICK LICK
Q.44

OK BOOT — JUS' TO SHOW THERE ARE NO HARMFUL EFFECTS WE'LL HAVE A BATH TOGETHER — RIGHT ?
Q.45
AN' WE'LL DO IT IN STAGES
— I'LL PUT ONE FOOT IN AN' YOU PUT ONE FOOT IN
NOW BOTH FEET
. . . TO BE FOLLOWED BY YOUR WHOLE BODY
YOU LOOK RIDICULOUS — IF YOU ONLY KNEW HOW RIDICULOUS . . .

COME ON BOOT — YOU MANAGED TO GET TWO FEET IN WITHOUT EXPIRIN' — SO GET IN
Q.46
AN' SIT DOWN — FOR GOODNESS SAKE SIT DOWN
CRUMBS WHAT NOW ? WHAT COULD POSSIBLY BE BOTHERIN' YOU NOW ?
HOW ABOUT A MARKED AVERSION TO PROVIDING ACCOMMODATION FOR YOUR BIG TOE ?

WELL YOU DID IT AT LAST — YOU GOT YOURSELF INTO THE BATH AT LAST
ALTHOUGH WHAT SWAYED YOU IN THE END I DO NOT KNOW
NOR DO I
BUT I KNOW WHAT *DIDN'T*
Q.47

CRUMBS BOOT— WE WEREN'T HALF DIRTY
LOOK AT THIS WATER— JUS' *LOOK* AT IT
IT'S *ALIVE*— IT'S *SEETHIN'*
I WONDER IF WE COULD *BOTTLE* IT?
Q.48

THERE Y'ARE, BOOT — THAT'S ABOUT AS DRY AS I C'N GET YOU FOR THE TIME BEING
Q.49
— I'LL GO AN' FIND MYSELF SOME CLOTHES
FUNNY THING — THAT
I'M NOT ALLOWED TO WALK ABOUT IN MY BIRTHDAY SUIT — BUT YOU CAN
I S'POSE THERE'S A REASON FOR THAT
PRECISELY
I DON'T LOOK ABSOLUTELY APPALLING IN MINE

YOU'RE STILL A BIT DAMP AFTER YOUR BATH BOOT
Q.50
I'M GOIN' TO HAVE TO USE THE HAIR-DRYER ON YOU
LOOK, BOOT, WE'RE NOT GOIN' TO HAVE TO GO THROUGH ALL . . . OH, VERY WELL
STICK'M UP, Y'DIRTY RAT — I GOT Y'COVERED
THOUGH WHY Y'CAN'T BE DRIED OFF LIKE ANY OTHER DOG I DO NOT KNOW

HOLD STILL BOOT— YOU'RE NEARLY DRY—YOU'RE COMIN' UP A TREAT
Q.51
JUST A FEW MORE PUFFS FOR THE FINISHIN' TOUCH
THERE Y'ARE — YOU LOOK GREAT
THE ONLY THING IS — DON'T WANDER TOO NEAR TO ANY CANDY-FLOSS STALLS
?
HE HAS A STRANGELY OBSCURE SENSE OF HUMOUR DOES THAT BOY

CANDY-FLOSS ? WHAT CAN THIS LAD BE TALKING ABOUT ?
Q.52
AAGH
WHO IS THAT ? WHAT IS THAT ? IT SURELY CAN'T BE ME ?
EVEN IF IT WAS ME — HOW COULD I TELL ?
I CAN'T EVEN TELL IF THERE'S ANYBODY IN THERE
— ADMIRIN' THE FRUITS OF MY LABOUR, BOOT ? AT LAST I'VE GOT A NICE CLEAN DOG
BE THAT AS IT MAY
WHAT I'VE GOT IS AN IDENTITY CRISIS

WHERE AM I ? WHAT AM I ? AM I SOMEWHERE WITHIN THIS AMORPHOUS MASS ?
Q.53
THERE'S SURELY AN ANSWER TO ALL THESE QUESTIONS
I KNOW WHAT I'LL DO — I'LL HAVE A BIT OF A THINK
WELL —THAT'S AS GOOD A THINK AS I'VE HAD IN MANY A LONG YEAR
BUT HOW CAN I FIT THE CONCEPT OF '*THE EVERLASTING SAUSAGE*' INTO THIS CURRENT SITUATION ?

THE THOUGHT OF '*THE EVERLASTING SAUSAGE*', BRILLIANT THOUGH IT MAY BE, IS OF DOUBTFUL VALUE IN THIS CURRENT SITUATION
Q.54
WHICH IS, IN ITSELF, A PRETTY GOOD THOUGHT BY THE LORD HARRY— YOU'RE IN CRACKING GOOD FORM TODAY, BOOT
AND IF I'VE ***THOUGHT*** ALL THOSE THOUGHTS I MUST BE SOMEWHERE INSIDE HERE ***THOUGHTING*** ALL THESE ***THINKS***
I MEAN — THINKING ALL THESE THOUGHTS
AND THAT'S YET ANOTHER THOUGHT I'VE THUNK
I THINK
OH DEUCE TAKE IT
I SHOULD'VE STOPPED AT '*THE EVERLASTING SAUSAGE*'

WELL AT LEAST I KNOW I'M IN HERE SOMEWHERE — BUT WHICH END IS WHICH
Q.55
YET AGAIN THE DOG'S SEARING INTELLECT IS BROUGHT TO BEAR
WELL... THIS END IS THIS END
AND THAT END IS THAT END
AND IF THAT END DOESN'T START DOING ITS SHARE OF THE THINKING THERE'S GOING TO BE TROUBLE

HAVING ESTABLISHED I'M IN HERE SOMEWHERE —AND THAT THERE ARE TWO ENDS TO IT
Q.56
I HAVE TO ASCERTAIN WHICH END I'M AT—WHICH END'S THE H.Q. WHAT ?
DAMME BUT ONCE ONE STARTS THIS THINKING LARK THERE SEEMS NO END TO IT
I'VE GOT IT—I'LL PRESENT THAT END TO THE MIRROR
CAN YOU SEE ANYTHING FROM THAT END OLD CHAP ?
— NO I CAN'T
CAN YOU SEE ANYTHING FROM THIS END DEAR HEART ?
OF COURSE I CAN YOU FOOL
THIS END MAY BE GIFTED BUT IT'S GIVEN TO INSUBORDIN-ATION

I'VE NOW REASONED OUT WHO I AM AND WHERE I AM
I'M ME — I'M IN HERE — AND I'M AT THIS END OF HERE
Q.57
BY THE LORD HARRY — THE DEAR DOG'S INTELLECTUAL POWER DEFIES... WAIT... HOLD HARD CULLY
IF I'M AT THIS END — WHAT'S AT THAT END?
AND WHY'S IT FOLLOWING ME?
WELL LET'S SEE IF AN INVESTIGATIVE BITE WILL PROVIDE THE ANSWER
YIPE
THAT END'S GOT SOME PRETTY SNEAKY ACCOMPLICES

BY THE LORD HARRY — HERE'S A HOW-DE-DO
THAT END'S DOGGING MY FOOTSTEPS
Q.58
AND IS IN LEAGUE WITH SECRET ALLIES
WELL — MUCH AS IT GOES AGAINST THE GRAIN A STRATEGIC WITHDRAWAL IS INDICATED
OR IN THE MILITARY PARLANCE OF MY REGIMENT, O'BUNION'S INTRUDERS — RUN LIKE THE CLAPPERS
DEY-VIL TAKE IT
IT'S TRYING FOR A TAKE-OVER

BY THE LORD HARRY, SIRRAH — CEASE FOLLOWING ME OR YOU'LL FEEL THE BITE OF CAPTAIN BOOT — OF O'BUNION'S INTRUDERS!
Q.59
HAUL OFF! DESIST!
VERY WELL THEN — ON YOUR OWN HEAD (OR WHATEVER) BE IT
HAVE AT THEE
YIPE
GRRR
NO QUARTER
WHAT'S THE MEANING OF THIS?
— A SILLY QUESTION TO WHICH ANY KIND OF ANSWER IS EXTREMELY UNLIKELY

LOOK AT THE MESS YOU'VE MADE YOU DOPEY DOG
Q.60
I'VE SEEN YOU DO SOME DAFT THINGS, BOOT, BUT HONESTLY — CHASIN' ABOUT AFTER YOUR OWN REAR
MY OWN REAR? SO THAT'S WHY THAT END WAS FOLLOWING ME
IT NEVER SAID
I SUPPOSE IT'S NOT VERY BRIGHT
JUST AS WELL I SUPPOSE
IF *THAT* END STARTED *THINKING*, IT MIGHT WANT SOME OF THE *BENEFITS* ENJOYED BY *THIS* END
— AND THERE'S NOT ENOUGH TO GO ROUND

I MAY NOT LOOK LIKE THE OLD ME BUT I AM THE OLD ME
AND 'TIS A GREAT RELIEF AND NO MISTAKE KNOWING IT IS ALL ME IN HERE
DEUCE TAKE IT — 'TWERE A RARE VEXATION FOR A TIME
NOT ONLY NOT KNOWING WHO I WAS BUT WHICH END I WAS
RIGHT, BOOT, I'M TAKING YOU OUT TO SHOW EVERYBODY MY NICE CLEAN DOG
OH NOW DON'T YOU START
Q.61

'LO WELLIN'TON 'LO BOOT
COR — DOZEN 'E LOOK CLEAN
'lo wellin'ton 'lo boot
crumbs — you do look clean
LITTLE DO PEOPLE REALISE HOW WOUNDING THE CHANCE REMARK CAN BE
Q.62

'LO WELLIN'TON — 'LO BOOT
CRUMBS — DOESN'T HE LOOK **CLEAN** FOR A CHANGE
Q.63
YEA, WELL — Y'SEE I GAVE HIM A BATH — IT WAS A STRUGGLE — A REAL DRAMA BUT WORTH IT IN THE END AN'...
WHAT **ARE** YOU GOIN' **ON** ABOUT ?
— I WAS **NOT** REFERRIN' TO OLE BOOT

WELL, BOOT, PEOPLE WERE CERTAINLY SURPRISED AND DELIGHTED BY THE NEW 'SQUEAKY-CLEAN' YOU
Q.64
THOUGH I MUST SAY — YOU DIDN'T SEEM ALL THAT HAPPY ABOUT IT
GIVEN YOUR OWN WAY YOU'D RATHER GO AN' ROLL IN SOME OLE HEAP OF RUBBISH
AN' COME UP SMELLIN' OF SOMETHIN' OTHER THAN CHANEL NUMBER 5
I HAVE A GIFT FOR SENSING THAT SORT OF THING — DON'T ASK ME HOW

VROOM VROOM-VROOM VAROOM
OOOM OOOM OOOM BRRR BRRR ROOOM
RMMM RMMM VROOM !AOOOOW WOWOWOWO....
ARE WE THERE YET ?
Q.65

I HAD A THOUGHT THE OTHER DAY B.H.—ONE OF MY BETTER THOUGHTS
I THOUGHT OF AN *EVERLASTING SAUSAGE*
BY JINGO, BOOT OLD FRUIT, WHAT A PERFECTLY FIRST-CLASS TOP-HOLE REMARKABLE THOUGHT
—WHO MAKES THEM ?
NOBODY MAKES THEM —IT WAS JUST SOMETHING I THOUGHT
AH—BUT IF YOU ***THOUGHT*** OF IT— IT POSSIBLY EXISTS
AN IDEA ENCAPSULATED IN THE SAYING *'WHAT THE MIND CAN CONCEIVE THE WILL CAN ACHIEVE'*
BY THE LORD HARRY— THAT'S PRETTY GOOD—WHO THOUGHT OF IT ?
I DID— IT'S MY OWN PERSONAL PROPERTY ©B.H. (CALCUTTA) Failed. 1982
—IT'S MUCH TOO GOOD FOR THE LIKES OF YOU
Q.66

ARE YOU SURE YOU THOUGHT THAT THOUGHT — *'WHAT THE MIND CAN CONCEIVE THE WILL CAN ACHIEVE'*
Q.67
OF COURSE I'M SURE — WHAT ARE BEING WRONG WITH YOU ?
IT DOESN'T SEEM ETHNIC ENOUGH FOR YOU — NO OFFENCE MEANT
OH — MOST ASTONISHINGLY SORRY ABOUT THAT — I'LL ETHNIC IT UP A BIT FOR YOU
VAT DE MI-I-I-I-I-ND CAN CONCE-E-E-E-E-IVE DE VILL CAN ACHI-E-E-E-EVE
THERE'S NO NEED TO COME THE SARKY DARKIE

WOULD IT MOLLIFY YOU TO KNOW I THINK YOUR IDEA IS FIRST-RATE AND WORTHY OF DEVELOPMENT
Q.68
OH — SO NOW YOU'RE THINKING OF TAKING ADVANTAGE OF IT
NOT A BIT OF IT
I'M THINKING OF STEALING IT
I CAN SEE YOU'RE BEING ENTIRELY WITHOUT SCRUPLES
YOU CAN'T BE LOOKING AT THE RIGHT PLACE

ACCORDING TO YOUR THEORY B.H., IF I CAN THINK OF AN EVERLASTING SAUSAGE—IT MUST BE POSSIBLE TO MAKE ONE
PRECISEMENTS — PERHAPS SOMEBODY HAS
OH COME NOW —IF THEY HAD EVERYBODY WOULD HAVE ONE
NOT NECESSARILY — IT MIGHT BE LIKE THOSE OTHER THINGS —THE EVERLASTING LIGHT-BULB AND THE EVER-LASTING RAZOR-BLADE
Q.69
BY THE LORD HARRY—YOU KNOW WHAT THIS MEANS — THEY'VE SUPPRESSED IT
YOU MEAN— IT INTERFERED WITH T.V. RECEPTION ?

I WAS NOT TALKING OF T.V. RECEPTION WHEN I SAID THE 'EVERLASTING SAUSAGE' HAD BEEN SUPPRESSED
OH
I MEANT GAGGED, MUZZLED, MUFFLED, SMOTHERED, SAT ON
Q.70
SPOKE OUT OF TURN DID IT ?

Q.71
HOW LONG WOULD AN 'EVERLASTING SAUSAGE' LAST ?
A ?
WHAT ?
WELL — FOREVER — IT'S IMPLICIT IN THE NAME
(SNIFF) I BET THERE'S SOMETHING IN THE SMALL PRINT

Q.72
?
THERE'S ANOTHER THING WHICH WORRIES ME ABOUT THE 'EVERLASTING SAUSAGE'
AT WHICH END WOULD YOU START ?

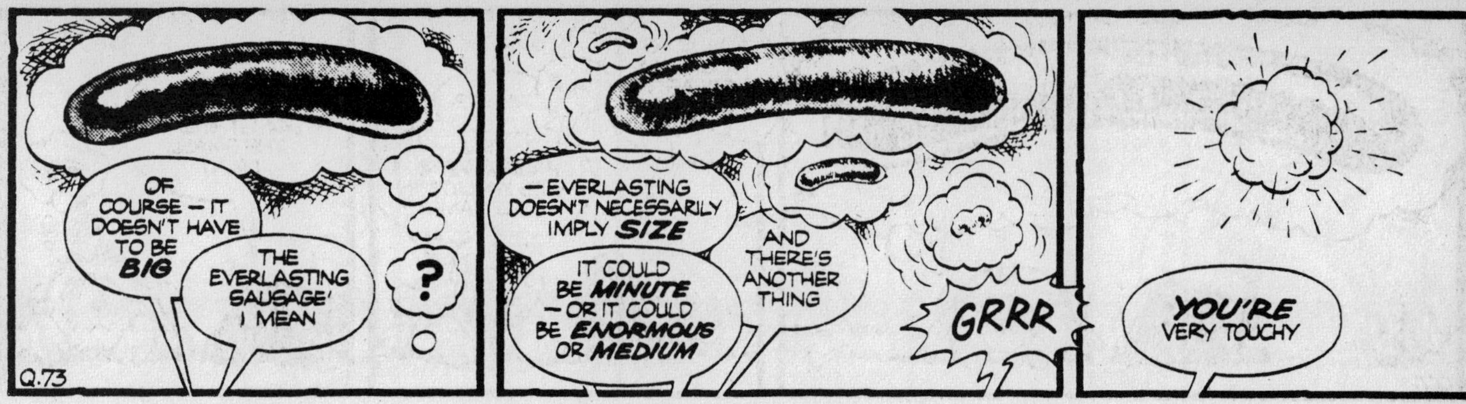
Q.73
OF COURSE – IT DOESN'T HAVE TO BE BIG
THE EVERLASTING SAUSAGE' I MEAN
?
– EVERLASTING DOESN'T NECESSARILY IMPLY SIZE
IT COULD BE MINUTE – OR IT COULD BE ENORMOUS OR MEDIUM
AND THERE'S ANOTHER THING
GRRR
YOU'RE VERY TOUCHY

Q.74
GOODNESS GRACIOUSNESS, BOOT – WHAT HAVE YOU GOT THERE ?
SAUSAGES
EVERLASTING ?
NO
?
– SHORT LIVED

WHENCE CAME THOSE REMARKABLY TRANSIENT SAUSAGES ?
BEN-THE-BUTCHER-IN-THE-HIGH-STREET
THE GAME IS YOU STAND IN HIS DOORWAY AND STARE AT HIM UNTIL HE BECOMES IRRITATED AND HE HURLS SAUSAGES AT YOU
Q.75
I MUST TRY MY HAND AT THIS SPLENDID GAME
I DON'T THINK HE UNDERSTANDS THE RULES

I AM HAVING A THEORY ABOUT THAT BEN-THE-BUTCHER-IN-THE-HIGH-STREET
DO TELL
Q.76
WELL WHEN HE OBSERVED YOU CASING HIS PREMISES HE TRIED TO BUY YOU OFF WITH A STRING OF SAUSAGES
AND WHEN I TOOK OVER SURVEILLANCE HE CHANGED TACTICS AND CONKED ME WITH A BONE
HE ARE SHOWING CLASSIC SYMPTOMS OF GUILT AND PANIC — I'M THINKING HE ARE HIDING SOMETHING
YOU MEAN....
THE EVERLASTING SAUSAGE
HEY, BEN, THOSE TWO DOGS ARE HERE AGAIN

HEY BEN, THOSE DOGS ARE HAUNTING THIS PLACE
—BUNG A COUPLE OF SHIN-BONES AT 'EM
THAT GOT RID OF 'EM
IF THEY COME BACK PRESENT THEM WITH THE BILL
HO-HO BEN — YOU ARE A....
ER ... BEN....

Q.77

WHO'D HAVE THOUGHT BEN-THE-BUTCHER COULD HAVE BEEN CAPABLE OF SUCH UNDERHAND RUTHLESSNESS
HE HAVE PROVED A GREAT DISAPPOINTMENT TO ME
I MEAN HEAVING A COUPLE OF HEFTY GREAT SHIN-BONES AT US WAS FAIR-FIGHTING — THE MANLY AND BRITISH THING TO DO
PRECISEMENTS
BUT TO COME AT US WITH THE STAFF COLLECTION BOX...
AND IT ARE NOT EVEN CHRISTMAS

Q.78

BOOT— I'VE HAD A REQUEST FROM BEN-THE-BUTCHER-IN-THE-HIGH-STREET
Q.79
—THAT YOU STOP HANGIN' AROUN' HIS SHOP
OH I DIDN'T TAKE IT LYIN' DOWN — I STOOD UP FOR YOU
HOW D'YOU KNOW IT'S OLE BOOT ? I SAID -- HOW D'YOU KNOW IT'S DEAR OLE BROWN-EYES ?
OR, TO BE QUITE ACCURATE — DEAR OLE ONE-BROWN-AN'-ONE-BLUE-EYES
BUT HE'S GOT YOUR DESCRIPTION — RIGHT ON THE NAIL
YOU **ARE** THE 'SCRUFFY OLE FLEA-TRAP WHO'S BEEN DEVALUIN' HIS FRONTAGE' AREN'T YOU ?

I'M CONVINCED THE EVERLASTING SAUSAGE **EXISTS**
Q.80
BUT THIS GREAT BOON TO DOGMANITY HAS BEEN **SUPPRESSED**
BY A SINISTER CARTEL OF BANGER-BARONS WHO...
SHUSH, BOOT— **HUSH** FOR GOODNESS SAKE
—**WALLS** HAVE EARS

ANY LINGERING DOUBTS ANYONE MAY HAVE CONCERNING THE EXISTENCE OF THE EVERLASTING SAUSAGE OUGHT TO BE DISPELLED BY THIS
WHO D'YOU THINK MODELLED FOR THAT
I'm meaty. Fry me."
Wall's
Q.81

HEY BOOT— KNOW WHAT'S IN MY DIARY FOR TODAY?
THE EVERLASTING SAUSAGE: VITAL STATISTICS
IT SAYS 'HILARY LAW SITTINGS END'
BUT WHO IS HILARY LAW? WHY IS SHE ENDING HER SITTINGS? COME TO THAT WHY DID SHE START SITTING IN THE FIRST PLACE?
THEY NEVER TELL YOU THESE THINGS
THERE ARE TIMES WHEN I FIND THE ADULT WORLD COMPLETELY INCOMPREHENSI-BABBLE
IF EINSTEIN HAD HAD THESE CONSTANT INTERRUPTIONS HE'D NEVER HAVE INVENTED RELATIVES
Q.82

OF COURSE—THE 'EVERLASTING SAUSAGE' MAY NOT BE A PHYSICAL ENTITY AT ALL— IT MAY BE A MYSTICAL MANIFEST-ATION
A?
Q.83
WE MAY WELL BE PURSUING SOMETHING OF TRANSCENDENTAL SYMBOLISM—AS WITH THE HOLY GRUEL
GRAIL YOU NITWIT— ***GRAIL***
BY THE LORD HARRY— WHAT AILS THE FELLOW?
DEUCE TAKE IT, B.H., WHAT ***ARE*** YOU DOING?
I'M ***GRAILING***
I THINK
MIND YOU—IT'S SO LONG SINCE LAST I GRAILED I'VE ALMOST FORGOTTEN HOW IT'S DONE

LISTEN, B.H. (CALCUTTA) Failed — WHAT YOU'RE DOING IS KNOWN IN THE TRADE AS STANDING ON YOUR STUPID HEAD
WHAT YOU'RE ***NOT*** DOING IS ***GRAILING***— THERE'S NO SUCH THING AS GRAILING
Q.84
WHYFOR THEN DID YOU URGE ME TO DO IT—IN TONES OF EXTREME URGENCY
I WAS MERELY POINTING OUT THE MYSTICAL CONCEPT YOU REFERRED TO AS THE HOLY GRUEL WAS, IN FACT, THE HOLY GRAIL
GRAIL, NOT ***GRUEL***— WHICH HAPPENS TO BE A THIN LIQUID COLLATION MADE BY BOILING OATMEAL OR SOME OTHER FARINACEOUS SUBSTANCE
I CAN SEE RIGHT UP YOUR NOSE

SO YOU THINK THE 'EVERLASTING SAUSAGE' MAY BE A CONCEPT OF A TRANSCENDENTAL NATURE ?
PRECISEMENTS
Q.85
— AN IDEAL AFTER WHICH TO STRIVE, THUS STRENGTHENING THE CHARACTER, REFINING THE MIND AND ENNOBLING THE SOUL
THAT ARE SOUNDING LIKE THE CORRECT SPECIFICATIONS
— LET'S HOPE LIKE MAD IT'S JUST SOMETHING TO EAT

. . . BAXTERS, BOWYERS, DEWFRESH, FORTNUM & MASON, HARRODS, MARKS & SPENCER, HARRIS, McKELLER, MILLER, PALETHORPE, RICHMOND, SAINSBURY, WALLS —AND ALL YE MIGHTY MEN OF MEATITUDE
Q.86
VOUCHSAFE A VISION OF THE EVERLASTING SAUSAGE, (WITH PERHAPS A GENEROUS FREE SAMPLE) TO YOUR HUMBLE DEVOTEE, BOOT (LORD BOOT AS WAS AND LATE CAPTAIN BOOT OF O'BUNION'S INTRUDERS)
PLOP
HEY YOU LOT, I ASKED FOR A BANGER — NOT A WHIMPER

LET'S TRY AGAIN O LORDS OF THE SAUSAGE
I CONJURE THEE BY WISH-BONE, THIGHBONE, SHINBONE AND BY THE LORD HARRY
VOUCH-SAFE TO ME A **GENEROUS TOKEN** OF...
5p off
THE INCANTATION GAME ISN'T WORTH A DAMN THESE DAYS
Q.87

HOLD HARD, BACK UP, A THOUGHT OCCURS
THE SAUSAGE I CONJURED – 'TWAS NOT VERY LARGE – BUT IF 'TWERE **THE EVERLASTING SAUSAGE...**
IT WOULDN'T **NEED** TO BE – **SIZE** WOULD BE OF **NO CONSEQUENCE**
IT'S STILL HERE – **NOW** WE'LL SEE IF IT'S...
EVERLASTING
ALL RIGHT – **ALL RIGHT** – TECHNICALLY IT'LL NEVER GET EATEN BUT I STILL SAY IT'S A SHABBY TRICK
Q.88

YOU'RE MEANING THERE REALLY ARE AN EVERLASTING SAUSAGE ?
YES— I'VE CONJURED IT ONCE—IT'S WORTH A SECOND TRY
Q.89
AND IT ARE OF A TRANSIENT NATURE — LIKE THE HOLY GRUEL
GRAIL— GRAIL
NOW — WE'LL GIV'M BOTH BARRELS — CONCENTRATE AND WISH
YOU AND YOUR BLASTED HOLY GRUEL

BOOT OLD CHAPPIES— ARE THERE ANY MORE DEVELOPINGS REGARDING THE EVERLASTING SAUSAGE ?
A?... OH.... BOTHER ME NOT WITH THAT TISH-TOSHERY, B. H.
Q.90
I REALISE NOW'TWAS BUT A VAIN AND SILLY THING
A CONCEIT— AN IDLE DREAM —A FOLLY
I NOW HAVE SOME-THING CONSIDERABLY WEIGHTIER TO OCCUPY MY MIND
SIC TRANSIT GLORIA SALSICIUM
THE EVERLASTING BONE : VITAL STATISTICS

RIGHT—BERYL— Y'READY ?—LET'R GO
VOTES FOR GIRLS—VOTES
OH CRUMBS
FOR GIRLS VOTES
NO, BERYL, NO—I WANT Number 6
NO HOME-WORK WITHOUT UNION RATES
THAT'S Number 5 —I WANT Number 6
MMERM MM
NO HOMEWORK WITHOU
I *KNEW* I SHOULD'VE KEPT IT ALL TO ONE HAND
Q.91

Y'CAN'T GET IT WRONG *NOW* BERYL—SO LET'S HAVE IT
NO HOMEWORK WITHOUT
NO—*NO*—BERYL—LOOK —I WANT Number 6
PUT GLUE ON THE NATIONAL
NO NO—LOOK BERYL Number 6
MAISIE FOR MAY QUEEN
THAT'S *IT* BERYL—MARVELLOUS, MAGIC, VERY GOOD
NOW LET'S TRY IT *WITHOUT* THE PROMPT-BOARD
6 MAISIE FOR MAY QUEEN
Q.92

RIGHT YOU LOT—PAY ATTENTION AN' FACE THE FRONT
Q.93
MAISIE FOR MAY QUEEN —REPEAT AFTER ME
JUSTA MINUTE MAISIE—WOT'S THE BOARD FOR?
IT'S A PROMPT BOARD—SPECIALLY MADE FOR THOSE WHO HAVEN'T GOT THE MESSAGE
YOU MUST THINK WE'RE STUPID—SPECIALLY IF YOU THINK WE'RE GONNA STAN' 'ERE RABBITIN' SILLY SLOGANS FOR YOUR BENEFIT...
YOU OBVIOUSLY NEED A BIT OF PROMPTING

MAISIE-FOR-MAY-QUEEN MAISIE-FOR-MAY-QUEEN HAVE YOU GOT THE MESSAGE YET, MARLON?
Q.94
RIGHT MAISIE—THAT'S IT—NOW I'VE GOT A MESSAGE FOR YOU YOU STUPID KID
I TAKE IT YOU HAVE MET BERYL BOGEY—THE ALL-IN FREE-STYLE BLACK-BELT WOMAN'S LIBERATED...
...NETBALL CHAMPION

AM I RIGHT TO ASSUME I C'N COUNT ON YOUR TOTAL SUPPORT FOR MAISIE AS MAY QUEEN WHEN
MAISIE — THIS IS NO WAY....
WOT'RE YOU STANDIN' THERE RABBITIN' ABOUT, WELLIN'TON ? DO SOMETHIN' — YOU'RE SUPPOSED TO BE MY BES' FRIEN'
Q.95
OOH — OUCH — EEK
KEEP IN STEP — IT HELPS IF YOU KEEP IN STEP

THAT ROTTEN MAISIE AN' HER BERYL-BOGEY BLACK-BELT NETBALL CHAMPION
D'YOU THINK SHE'LL GET MANY VOTES ?
I DUNNO
— SHE'S CERTAINLY CAMPAIGNIN' HARD ENOUGH
Q.96

YEA-BOO -RATBAG- SAME TO YOU
THRUPPP
Q.97
I TOLD YOU HE WOULDN'T LET US ON THAT BUS

YOU'LL STAY TILL MY MUM ANSWERS THE DOOR, WON'T YOU WELLIN'TON ?
WHY ?
TO HELP TELL WOT HAPPENED, O'COURSE
I DUNNO —I MEAN, SHE WON'T BE VERY PLEASED
CRUMBS — ALL I WANT IS A BIT OF BACK-UP — A BIT OF THE OLE MORAL SUPPORT— IS THAT TOO MUCH TO ASK ?
OH ALL RIGHT MARLON
I'LL RING THE BELL
ER... MUM...
WELLIN'TON'S GOT SOMETHIN' TO TELL YOU
Scorpio
Q.98

MAISIE FOR MAY QUEEN — MAISIE FOR MAY QUEEN
RIGHT — LET'S HAVE A SHOW OF HANDS
Q.99
OR — FAILIN' THAT...
♫
BERYL
— WE'LL HAVE A SHOW OF KNUCKLES

MAISIE — WE'VE ALL GOT TOGETHER TO 'AVE A WORD WITH YOU ABOUT YOUR METHOD OF GETTIN' VOTES
YEA — AN' WE WANT A WORD WITH THAT BERYL BOGEY, TOO
MAISIE FOR MAY-QUEEN CAMPAIGN HEADQUARTERS
Q.100
BERYL BOGEY CANNOT BE DISTURBED RIGHT NOW
— SHE'S EATIN' A GUARD-DOG
R MAY-QUEEN HEADQUARTERS

BUT WHAT HAPPENED? I STILL DON'T UNDERSTAND WHAT HAPPENED?
Q.101
WELL Y'SEE — IN ORDER TO IMMOBILISE BLOSSOM McGINSBERG'S SUPPORTERS FROM VOTIN'
MAISIE WENT AN' SMEARED GLUE ON THE LOO SEATS
AN' THEN, ABSENTMINDEDLY...
GIRLS
HAS ANYONE SENT FOR MY MUM?

WELL I ONLY HOPE YOU'VE LEARNED YOUR LESSON
YEA
Q.102
YOU THOUGHT THAT WITH YOUR BULLYIN' AN' UNDERHAND TRICKS YOU'D END UP AS QUEEN OF THE MAY
YEA
'STEAD OF WHICH YOU ENDED UP AS QUEEN OF THE LOO — WITH A SEAT STUCK TO YOUR REAR
RIGHT
WOULD YOU MIND KEEPIN' YOUR VOICE DOWN — WOULD YOU MIND?
WHAT'RE YOU TRYIN' TO DO — MAKE A SPECTACLE OF ME?

CRUMBS — LOOK AT THE BUS QUEUE
WE'RE GONNA HAFTA WAIT FOR HOURS
Q.103
HANG ABOUT — HERE COMES DIRTY McSQUIRTY
HULLO ALOYSIOUS, DEAR OLE FRIEN' — HAVEN'T SEEN YOU FOR HOURS
YEA — HOW'VE YOU BEEN?
HOW LONG HAVE I BEEN A VALUED AND LIFELONG FRIEND?
UNTIL THE NEXT BUS

— GREAT IDEA OF YOURN — TEAMIN' UP WITH DIRTY McSQUIRTY
YEA — THE KIDS ALWAYS LET HIM TO THE FRONT OF THE QUEUE
Q.104
ER TRAVEL
— THE THING I FORGOT WAS
— THEY NEVER LET HIM ON THE BUS

WHERE'RE YOU GOIN', DIRTY McSQUIRTY ?
TO VISIT COUSIN WORSOFF
THE SOMEONE WORSOFF WHO'S ALWAYS THAN YOURSELF ?
THE VERY SAME
I THINK HE'S AROUN' HERE SOMEWHERE — HE'S JUST CHANGED DRAINS
OH ? WHAT WAS WRONG WITH THE OLD DRAIN ?
THE NEIGHBOURHOOD WAS GOIN' DOWNHILL
Q.105

THE NEIGHBOURHOOD WAS GOIN' DOWNHILL ?
YOUR COUSIN WAS LIVIN' IN A ***DRAIN***— AN' ***MOVED*** BECAUSE THE ***NEIGHBOURHOOD*** WAS GOIN' ***DOWN-HILL ?***
IS THIS SOME KIND OF A JOKE ?
IT'S NO JOKE I CAN ASSURE YOU
HOW WOULD ***YOU*** FANCY FOUR BREAK-INS WITHIN A COUPLE OF MONTHS ?
Q.106

YOU THINK THIS IS THE NEW DRAIN YOUR COUSIN WORSOFF HAS MOVED INTO ?
YES — I'LL GIVE HIM A SHOUT
ARE YOU THERE COUSIN WORSOFF ?
THIS IS A RECORDED MESSAGE
COUSIN WORSOFF REGRETS HE'S NOT AT HOME, BUT IF YOU'D LIKE TO LEAVE A MESSAGE
— ON THE BACK OF AN OLD CIGARETTE PACKET AND SUSPEND IT FROM THE THIRD GRATING FROM THE RIGHT...
Q.107

THIS IS A RECORDED MESSAGE — PLEASE LEAVE YOUR
JUST TO SAY ALOYSIOUS McSQUIRTY CALLED AND....
DIRTY McSQUIRTY! HEY — THIS ISN'T REALLY A RECORDED MESSAGE — THIS IS ME — COUSIN WORSOFF
I WAS ONLY PRETENDIN' TO BE A RECORDER 'CAUSE I THOUGHT YOU MIGHT BE THE BAILIFF
— COME TO REPOSSESS MY JAM-JAR
Q.108

DID HE SAY THEY'RE GOIN' TO REPOSSESS HIS JAM-JAR ?
THA'S WHAT HE SAID
WHY'RE THEY REPOSSESSIN' YOUR JAM-JAR COUSIN WORSOFF ?
I COULDN'T KEEP UP THE PAYMENTS
I TOOK ON TOO MUCH THERE, YOU KNOW
I SHOULD NEVER HAVE ORDERED THE OPTIONAL EXTRA PIECE OF STRING
Q.109

WHAT WITH ONE THING AND ANOTHER YOUR COUSIN WORSOFF MAY WELL BE THE SOMEBODY WHO'S ALWAYS WORSE OFF THAN YOURSELF
BUT HE IS — I KEEP TELLING YOU HE IS
LISTEN COUSIN WORSOFF — APART FROM EVERYTHING ELSE — HOW ARE YOU YOURSELF ?
OH .... AS BAD AS CAN BE EXPECTED
Q.110

COUSIN WORSOFF — I'VE BROUGHT ALONG A COUPLE OF FRIENDS AND ....
YOU'RE NOT THINKING OF COMING IN ARE YOU ? —
I HAVEN'T CLEANED UP AFTER THE PARTY — THE PLACE IS IN A TERRIBLE MESS
YOU HAD A PARTY, COUSIN WORSOFF ?
NO ... IT WAS THREE BLOCKS UP THE ROAD
Q.111

WELL LISTEN, COUSIN WORSOFF, IF WE CAN'T COME IN PERHAPS WE CAN ALL GO FOR A WALK — WOULD YOU LIKE THAT ?
GOOD IDEA — I COULD DO WITH A BIT OF FRESH AIR
NICE DAY FOR IT — DON'T YOU THINK ?
Q112

WHAT DOES YOUR COUSIN WORSOFF DO DOWN THE DRAIN ?
HE'S SEARCHING
SEARCHING ? SEARCHING FOR WHAT ?
THE MEANING OF LIFE
HE SPENDS ALL DAY DOWN THE DRAIN SEARCHING FOR THE MEANING OF LIFE ?
WELL — HE SPENDS A LOT OF TIME RESEARCHING
AH — SIFTING THROUGH BITS OF ARCANE AND ESOTERIC KNOWLEDGE
NO — IN HIS CIRCUMSTANCES JUST SIFTING THROUGH BITS
I WISH YOU LOT WOULDN'T TALK ABOUT ME AS IF I WEREN'T HERE
Q.113

IT DOZEN SEEM MUCH OF A LIFE YOUR COUSIN WORSOFF LEADS
— SPENDIN' ALL HIS TIME DOWN A DRAIN SEARCHIN' FOR THE MEANIN' OF LIFE
OH — HE'S ALSO A COLLECTOR
A COLLECTOR ?
OH YES — A COLLECTOR OF NOTE
HIS IS PROBABLY THE WORLD'S LARGEST COLLECTION OF CORRUG-ANT DEHYDRATED CITRUS COVERINGS
CRUMBS
MY GHAST IS SUITABLY FLABBERED
EUREKA !
I'VE GOT TO LEAVE YOU NOW
I'VE COME ACROSS THE MOST MARVELLOUS PIECE OF INTERESTINGLY WRINKLED OLD ORANGE PEEL
Q.114

LISTEN — DIRTY McSQUIRTY — IS THAT WHAT YOUR COUSIN WORSOFF COLLECTS...
...WRINKLED OLE BITS OF ORANGE PEEL ?
G'BYE COUSIN WORSOFF
Q.115
INTERESTINGLY WRINKLED BITS OF OLD ORANGE PEEL
HIS IS PROBABLY THE WORLD'S LARGEST COLLECTION
AN' PROBABLY THE WORLD'S ONLY COLLECTION
HE'S SEARCHIN' FOR A SUITABLE PLACE TO EXHIBIT HIS UNIQUE CUMULATION
Y'MEAN...
A MUSEUM ?
NO
— A TIP

WOT'S ALL THE EXCITEMENT ABOUT ?
— THE DETAILS OF THE SCHOOL FÊTE
SCHOOL N ICE BOARD
RHUBARB
RHUBARB
RHUBARB
RHUBARB
Q.116
WHY'RE YOU TALKIN' WITH AN IRISH ACCENT ?
IRISH ACCENT ? WHAT'RE YOU BABBLIN' ABOUT ?
THESE 'ERE SCHOOL FEET
FÊTE — NOT FEET FÊTE — FÊTE FÊTE — AS IN FESTIVAL, CARNIVAL, BEANO — JAMBOREE...
OH IT'S NO USE TRYIN' TO 'OLD A CONSERVATION WITH YOU
I C'N NEVER GET A WORD IN EDGEWAYS

WHERE Y'GOIN' MAISIE ?
—TO A MEETIN' OF, THE SCHOOL FÊTE STALLHOLDERS
I'LL COME WITH YOU
Y'CAN'T, MARLON, YOU'RE NOT A STALLHOLDER
CRUMBS — I ALREADY BELONG TO THE SAVE-OUR-FROGS APPEAL, THE CROWN-CORK-COLLECTORS' ASSOCERATION AN' THE PAT-A-DOG-A-DAY CLUB
HOW MANY ORGERISATIONS DOES A MAN HAVE TO JOIN TO GET A LOOK-IN IN THIS ROTTEN WORL'
Q.117

I HOPE YOU'VE ALL BROUGHT SOMETHING FOR THE VARIOUS STALLS AT THE SCHOOL FÊTE
PLACE YOUR DONATIONS IN THE APPROPRIATELY MARKED BOXES AT THE REAR OF THE HALL
Q.118
JUMBLE
OI!

... AND THEREFORE ON BEHALF OF MYSELF AND THE BOARD OF GOVERNORS I NOW DECLARE THIS SCHOOL FÊTE O-
-PEN
'RAY
NA-N'YA NA-N'YA NA-N'YA
YOU SHOULD'VE ***FOLLOWED*** THE ***INSTRUCTIONS*** — 'UPON DECLARING THE FÊTE OPEN — ***MOVE RAPIDLY ASIDE***
Q.119

WHERE'S THE CAKE STALL?
OVER BY THE FIRST-AID TENT
AN' ***THAT'S*** WHAT I CALL ***PLANNIN'***
Q.120

Q.121
GUESS THE WEIGHT OF THE CAKE, MARLON ?
GUESS the WEIGHT 5p
ER, MARLON — BEFORE YOU COME TO ANY SPECIFIC CONCLUSION
I INVITE YOU TO CONSIDER CERTAIN FACTS...

Y'KNOW THAT SAYIN' "Y'CAN'T HAVE YOUR CAKE AN' EAT IT"
Q.122
YEA
CAKE STALL
RIGHT HERE'S THE LIVIN' PROOF
CAKE STALL

LISTEN WELLIN'TON – I'M FED UP HEARIN' YOUR SNIDE REMARKS ABOUT OUR CAKE-STALL
AN' IF STANDIN' ABOUT WITH A GRIN AS SILLY AS YOUR REMARKS IS ALL..
HEY – MAISIE
— DO HURRY UP WITH THOSE ROCK-CAKES
Q.123

I'M GOIN' OVER TO THE SMASH-THE-CHINA STALL
YEA – IT'S GREAT FUN – Y'GOIN' TO HAVE A GO
NO – I'M GOIN' FOR SENTIMENTAL REASONS
IT BRINGS BACK MEMORIES OF YESTERYEAR
AN' FAMILY REUNIONS WITH AUNT ETHEL'S LOT
KERASH
Q.124

LARGE CARDBOARD BOX OF LOVE
5p
Q.125
CARDBOARD BOX?
WE COULDN'T AFFORD A TUNNEL
GIGGLE
SQUEAK
GIGGLE

I'D LIKE TO TRY IT—BUT I HAVEN'T GOT A PARTNER
WHY NOT GO IN AN' SEE WHAT TURNS UP?
LARGE CARDBOARD BOX OF LOVE
5p
URK-URK-URK
15p
TRY YOUR STRENGTH
15p
URK-URK-URK
Q.126

WHAT'S GOIN' ON IN THERE ?
WELL — IT WAS THE CARDBOARD BOX OF LOVE
BUT IT'S NOW THE LATEST THING IN 'TRY YOUR STRENGTH'
AAGH
URK-URK-URK-URK
BONK
AWK
Q.127
SOUNDS MORE LIKE A MASSACRE TO ME
AAAGH
UNC-UNC-UNC
EEK
ARE YOU MAN ENUFF FOR THE MASSACER 20p

RIGHT NEXT ONE PLEASE
UNC ?
GAH
Q.128
HOLD ON . . . JUST ONE MINUTE
UNC-UNC-UNC
UH ?
SORRY — THE LAST ONE ENJOYED IT SO MUCH HE'S DECIDED ON ANOTHER GO
AAGH

WE KNOW WHAT'S GOIN' ON IN THERE, MAISIE
—Y'GOT BERYL BOGEY WAITIN' TO BE KISSED
AN' YOU'RE SACRIFICIN' THE FLOWER OF THE SCHOOL'S YOUNG MANHOOD
AAGH
UNC-UNC-UNC
ARE YOU MAN ENUFF FOR THE MASSACER 20p
Q.129
WELL — WE'VE GOT A CUSTOMER FOR YOU
OH — COME ON — PLAY FAIR

I'M NOT LETTIN' DIRTY McSQUIRTY GO IN THERE
YOU'VE GOT TO — HIS MONEY'S THE SAME AS ANYBODY ELSE'S
UNC-UNC-UNC
GAH
Q.130
YOU'RE JOKIN'
?
IT DOESN' EVEN SMELL THE SAME

DON'T DO IT — DON'T **DO** IT
RIGHT THEN DIRTY McSQUIRTY OLE FRIEN' — GO IN THERE AN' TEACH THAT BERYL BOGEY A LESSON
URK URK
ARE YOU MAN ENUFF FOR THE MASSACER 20p
Q.131
URK URK URK ?
WHAT HAPPENED ?
I FORGOT — I SHOULD'VE TOLE HIM TO APPROACH FROM **DOWNWIND**
URK URK URK URK URK URK URK URK
ARE YOU MAN ENUFF FOR THE MASSACER 20p

H'LO BABY GRUMPLIN'
I'M TOLD YOU WON A GOLDFISH IN A BAG
AREN'T **YOU** THE LUCKY BOY ?
Q132
w-e-l-l ... the goldfish was all right i s'pose, maisie
— but i dint think much of the gravy

Q.133
PICK A STRAW 5p
CRUMBS, MARLON, CAN'T YOU DO *ANYTHIN'* RIGHT ?

Q.134
IS THERE AN ELECTRICIAN IN THE CROWD ?

...OF A CHILD ANSWERING TO THE NAME OF GRUMPLING COME TO THE ORGANISER'S TENT
... AND THAT'S THE FIFTH TIME HE'S BEEN BROUGHT IN TODAY — HOW MANY TIMES CAN ONE CHILD GET LOST ?
— AS MANY TIMES AS YOU'RE PREPARED TO GIVE HIM CHOC'LATE BISCUITS
Q.135

WHAT'S THIS ?
IT'S THE ROLL-A-TUPPENCE STALL
COO— I'LL HAVE TO HAVE A GO
I HAVEN'T WON ANYTHIN'— WHY HAVEN'T I WON ANYTHIN' ?
FOR A START YOU'VE GOT TO LET GO OF YOUR TUPPENCE
Q.136

LOOK, MAISIE, YOUR TUPPENCE IS SUPPOSED TO ROLL DOWN THAT CHUTE AN' IF IT LANDS IN A SQUARE, THEN YOU'LL **WIN**
Q.137
BUT Y'WON'T WIN **ANYTHIN'** IF Y'DON'T **LET GO** OF **YOUR** COIN
LET **GO** OF IT— Y'GOTTA **LET GO** OF IT
—LEND ME TUPPENCE

MAISIE—Y'GOTTA LET THAT TUPPENCE ROLL DOWN THE CHUTE—Y'GOTTA LET GO OF IT
WHY CAN'T YOU LET GO OF IT ?
Q.138
UNGRIP YOUR **FINGERS**— THAT'S **ALL** YOU'VE GOT TO DO
JUST **UNGRIP— LOOSEN UP— LET GO**
IS THERE A DOCTOR IN THE CROWD ?

Q.139
YOU'N YOUR TUPPENCE — I'VE NEVER SEEN ANYTHIN' SO MEAN IN MY LIFE
MEAN ? WHAT D'YOU MEAN — MEAN ?
I WAS JUS' SUFFERIN' FROM A SPASM — YOU HEARD WHAT THE DOCTOR SAID
ANYWAY I DID LET GO OF IT IN THE END
YEA — ONLY 'CAUSE THE DOCTOR HELD OUT FIVEPENCE IN EXCHANGE

THE PRIZES LOOK GOOD — I'LL HAVE A GO
HOW MANY BEANS IN THE JAR? 5p a go
1st
2nd
3rd
THIS IS GOIN' TO TAKE A BIT OF TIME
OI — JUST A MINUTE — WHAT'RE YOU DOIN' ?
COUNTIN' 'EM OF COURSE — WHAT ELSE ? 1... 2... 3...
YOU'RE S'POSED TO COUNT THEM IN THE JAR
DON'T BE STUPID — 'OW COULD I GET IN THAT LITTLE JAR ?
Q.140

1... 2... 3... ER... 4...
YOU'RE NOT S'POSED TO EMPTY THE BEANS **OUT** OF THE **JAR**– YOU'RE SUPPOSED TO COUNT 'EM WHEN THEY'RE **IN** THE JAR
'OW C'N I DO **THAT?** SOME O'THEM IS BEHIND THE OTHERS AN' SOME IS UNDERNEATH AN'...
THAT'S THE **WHOLE POINT** OF THE **GAME**
GAME?
5p A GO PUTS IT IN THE CATEGORY OF A DIABOLICAL FIDDLE
Q.141

OH ALL RI' THEN
SINCE I'VE PAID MY MONEY I'LL HAVE A GO AT COUNTIN' 'EM **IN** THE JAR
1..2...3...
4...5...6...
7... 8... HEY– I'VE GOTTA NIDEA
WHY DON'T YOU JUS' **TELL** ME HOW MANY THERE ARE?
HOW MANY BEANS IN THE JAR?
5p a go
1st
2nd
3rd
Q.142

Q.143
1...2...3...
HOW MANY BEANS IN THE JAR? 5p a go
4...5...6...
7...8...9... OH THIS IS HOPELESS — **HOPELESS**
WOT COMES AFTER 10 ?

I'VE JUS' HAD A GO AT THAT, MARLON — WHAT NUMBER DID YOU END UP WITH ?
15
15?
W-E-L-L... I HAVEN'T GOT ALL DAY
Q.144

Q.145
WHERE'S THAT MARLON ?
YEA — HE'S S'POSED TO BE HELPIN'
HE 'STINCTLY HEARD TEACHER SAY IT WAS TIME TO PACK UP
YOU'D THINK BEIN' A TEACHER, SHE'D CHOOSE HER WORDS MORE CAREFULLY
ZZZZZ

first of all, new baby, mum makes out a list
blob
but then she sees things which will come in handy, but which aren't on the list
gah
by the time she's piled in all the things which will come in handy but which aren't on the list the list has disappeared under the pile
glop
next day she discovers she hasn't got half the things which were on the list, so — she makes out a list
... it's called — shopping
berk
Q.146

of course, new baby, when we go shopping you get left outside for a quiet doze
glop
not me — i'm thrust into the thick of it
up and down the aisles in a swirling bobbing multicoloured whirl-pool of human-kind
and i have to make the most of such valuable social intercourse while i'm at the right age
geep
there'll come the day when i'll be too old for face to face meetings with all those kneecaps
berk
Q.147

mum got lost last time we went to the supermarket
blob
though i've **told** her to stay by me if my attention is diverted elsewhere — she wanders you know
glug
and some of those assistants are so **dense**...
— well i don't like making a scene, as you know
gah
but i had to behave in an **appalling** manner before anyone would go and look for her
berk
Q.148

SPECIAL
SPECIAL
Q.149
i ate a packet of biscuits before we got to the check-out —what did you do ?

OW LONG'VE WE BIN WALKIN'? I'M FOOTSORE AN' BLEEDIN'
ISN' THAT THE NAME OF A ADVERTISIN' AGENCY?
NAH - YOURE THINKIN' OF SNATCHY AN' SNATCHY
OR MAYBE IT WAS RUM AN' BUBBLY GUM
ANYWAY- WOT DO *YOU* KNOW ABOUT ADVERTISIN'?
I USED TO WORK IN A AGENCY- I 'AD THE TOBACCO ACCOUNT
Q150
YOU USED TO ADVERTISE TOBACCO?
NO- I WAS A TRAINEE WEEVIL- I USED TO *EAT* IT
KOF! KOF!

Q151
Y'MEAN YOU WERE A 'IGH-POWERED ADVERTISIN' EXHORTATIVE - IN CHARGE OF A TOBACCO ACCOUNT?
WIV A PLUSH ORIFICE AN' *FREE LUNCHEON VOUCHERS*?
YEA-I COINED SUMMA THE BEST KNOWN SLOGANS OF THE DAY
'SMOKA PACKA FAGSA DAY'
'A PACKA DAY KEEPS THE DOCTOR IN PAY'
'SMOKE A PIPE AN' WOMEN WIV A PECULIAR SENSE OF SMELL WILL FALL ALL OVER YOU'
IT'S WOT STARTED ME SMOKIN' - 'EAVILY
WELL WHY AIN'T YOU RICH AN' FAMOUS AN' LIVIN' IN THE LAP OF LAXATIVE?
I LORST THE ACCOUNT
KOF! KOF!
WHY WAS THAT?
I KEP' PASSIN' OUT DURIN' CLIENT MEETIN'S

D'JEW SAY BEIN' IN TOBACCO ADVERTISIN' IS WOT STARTED YOU SMOKIN'?
S'RIGHT
KOF! KOF!
S'FUNNY -I 'AD A COUSIN IN SOAP-BUT IT NEVER STARTED 'IM WASHIN'
WOT WOS 'E-A NEXECUTIVE?
NO-A CORPSE
'E FELL IN THE VAT
Q152

STOP-D'JEW SEE WOT I SEE?
AT THIS VERY MOMENT IN TIME I SEE WOT I'D RATHER NOT SEE
A BONE!
AN WHERE THERE'S A BONE...
THERE'S A RESIDUE OF 'UNDREDS O' BITS O' MICROSCOPIC NOURISHMENTS
-WHICH COULD FORM PART OF OUR CALORIE CONTROLLED DIET
Q153
GRONFF!
CHOMP!
BIT CHEWEY -INNIT?
BOING

IT FOUGHT BACK-THAT CRUMMY OLE BONE FOUGHT BACK
WELL NO CRUMMY BONE'S GONNA GET THE BETTER OF ME
Q154
GO ON-PUT THE BOOT IN-GIVE IT THE OLE RIGHT BOOT
HAR HAR-Y'PUT Y'R RIGHT FOOT IN..
Y'R RIGHT FOOT OUT

ACCEPT THIS TOKEN OF APPRECERATION FOR THE WAY YOU TACKLED THAT BONE - YOU USELESS ARTICLE
NEVER SEND A BOY TO DO A MAN'S JOB
I'M GOIN' TO DEAL WIV THAT COCKY BONE
YEA?
BIG-EAD
WELL YOU MIGHT 'AVE A SURPRISE COMIN' TO YOU
Q155
BOING
D'JEW 'EAR WOT I SAID? YOU MIGHT 'AVE A SURPRISE COMIN' TO...

'ELP ME -'ELP...
Q156
ME
AN' STOP FIDDLIN' WIV YER FLAMIN' 'AT

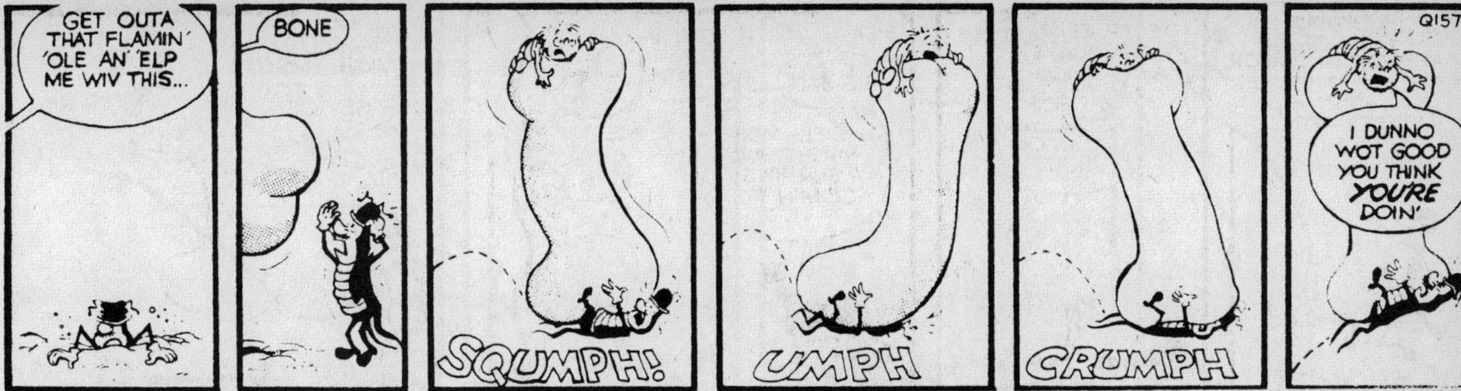
GET OUTA THAT FLAMIN' 'OLE AN' 'ELP ME WIV THIS...
BONE
SQUMPH!
UMPH
CRUMPH
Q157
I DUNNO WOT GOOD YOU THINK YOU'RE DOIN'

Q158
CRIPES
THIS IS LIKE BEIN'
ON A FLAMIN'
RUNAWAY BUS
DO SOMETHIN', USELESS
FARES PLEASE

FARES PLEASE?
WOT'RE YOU *TALKIN'* ABOUT – FARES PLEASE?
I 'AVEN'T GOT ANY FLAMIN' FARE
Q159
WELL I'M AFRAID YOU'LL 'AVE TO GET ORF

Q160
AAAGH
AND *WHAT* ARE *YOU TWO* DOING WITH *MY RUBBER BONE*?
RUBBER BONE? CRIPES – WE BIN CONNED
– TAKEN IN BY A SMOOTH-LOOKIN' *BOUNDER*

Q.161
I STILL WANT TO KNOW WHAT YOU TWO WRETCHES ARE DOING WITH MY RUBBER BONE
ER... WE'RE FROM THE MINISTRY OF RUBBER BONES
MINISTRY OF....? TISH AND TOSH, FELLOW
NO- NO—HONEST GUV—WE BIN CHECKIN' FOR HYSTERIA
Y'MEAN HYSTERESIS
GRRR
AAGH
YOU SPEAK FOR YOURSELF

'ELP 'ELP
A FINE FRIEN' YOU ARE
WELL THAT'S VERY NICE OF YOU TO SAY SO
Q.162
I WAS BEIN' SARCASTIC—WOT I REALLY THINK IS YOU'RE A RATBAG FOR RUNNIN' AWAY AN' LEAVIN' ME TO FACE THAT DOG
WELL WE LIVE AN' LEARN
I ALWAYS THOUGHT YOU WAS BRAVE AN' NEVER TOLD LIES
AN' I CAN'T STAND INSINCERITY

don't cry fur me Ar-chan-tina ♫
HEY-LOOK- IT'S ADOLPH - ADOLPH KILROY
Q.163
cheneral Kilroy if du bist not mindink
eim lookink fur some likely mugs —er lads
eim formink a hunta
WOT'SA HUNTA?
it's vas you'd call ein junta but those in der know pronounce der 'j' as ein 'h'
SOUNDS PRETTY POTTY
YEA— COUNT US OUT
der pickinks is good
WOT? BY HOVE— SOUNDS HUST THE HOB
YEA— WHATEVER IT IS YOU'RE HABBERIN' ON ABOUT

IT'S REAL HAMMY BELONGIN' TO A HUNTA
YEA— GETTIN' PAID HUST FOR SAYIN' 'H' INSTEAD OF 'J'— IT'S A HOY-RIDE
Q.164
ein moment señors— there's ein liddle more to it than that
to hustify your pay du might haft to fight
FIGHT? HUST— I MEAN JUST A MINUTE
YEA KILROY — Y'GOTTA BE HOKIN'— I MEAN JOKIN'
THIS JUNTA AIN'T OUR KINDA STUNTA

chust ein moment mein brave cabaleros
BRAVE? YOU'VE GOT THE WRONG CABALAY TURN
WE'RE BILLED AS THE COWARDY CUSTARDS— SHOW 'IM THE ACT
OH WE DON'T WANT TO FIGHT NO BY JINGO IT WON'T DO WE'D RATHER RUN— IT'S MUCH MORE FUN AN' MUCH MORE 'EALTHY TOO
don't you want to be brave soldiers of fortune?
SOLDIERS OF FORTUNE— YEA
IT'S BEIN' CORPSES OF FORTUNE WE CAN'T STAND
Q.165

nobody leaves der junta except by der sewers
WELL WE AIN'T FUSSY
WHERE'S THE NEAREST MAN'OLE COVER?
as mincemeat!
MINE YOU— I'M FUSSY ABOUT SOME THINGS— I'M NOT TOO KEEN ON MINCED CATERPILLAR
—AN' THE VERY THOUGHT OF CHOPPED BEETLE...
Q.166

OKAY — NOW WE'RE BACK IN THE JUNTA — WOT'S THE PAY ?
vell — it's not so much ein question of pay (dummkopfs)
it's more a share of der spoils
Q.167
COR — I AIN'T 'AD SPOILS FOR A LONG TIME
ME NEITHER
ER... WITH CHIPS ?
!

WHERE'S ALL THESE 'ERE SPOILS Y' WANT TAKEN, GENERAL ?
YEA — JUS' POINT THE WAY
we're goink to wrest das territory over there from das verdammt colonial englisher hundt
RIGHT NOW I DON'T NEED A WREST
Y'BETTER POINT THE OTHER WAY
Q.168
— while his back is turned
W-E-L-L — OK — BUT WREST ASSURED
YOU'RE GONNA LEAD THE WAY

undt now in defiance aufder imperialist (undt conveniently absent) englisher mutton-hundt ve vill der glorious emblem auf tortoisedom raise
RIGHT GUV
OLÉ
raise high der noble lettuce leaf
long may it stand as a sacred symbol auf defiance, nobility, justice (no, vait – cancel der justice) er...pride... nutrition... chlorophyll...
ER... KILROY...
WE GOT A BIT OF A PROBLEM
Q.169

undt now der noble symbol auf tortoisedom stands erect
let der plundering begin
YEA
WA-HOO
GRAB ALL – SPARE NONE
LET'S GO LET'S GO
how much plunder hast du amassed ?
WOT WE'VE AMASSED UP TO NOW IS A GREAT BIG PILE OF NOTHIN' (GASP – PANT)
YEA – WE'VE GRABBED ALL THE NOTHIN' WOT WAS AVAILABLE (PANT-GASP)
don't forget – ei'm taking 75%
Q.170

YOU'RE GONNA TAKE 75% OF OUR PLUNDER ?
WHICH WAS NOTHIN'
Q.171
WHICH LEAVES US LESS THAN NOTHIN'
THIS LIBERATIN' LARK AIN'T WORTH A CANDLE—WE'RE QUITTIN'
vait—ei'm changink mein mind—i'll settle for three-quarters
NOW YER TALKIN'
YEA—WE SURE CALLED 'IS BLUFF
THAT LEAVES 3/16 FER YEW AN' 1/16 FER ME
NO-NO-3/16 FER ME AN'...
NOTHIN' DOIN'—3/16 FER...
DO ME A FAVOUR IT'S...
hast du der agreement reached ?
YEA—I'M EMPOWERED TO SPEAK FOR MY PARTNER WHILE THE BALANCE OF HIS EYE-BALLS IS DISTURBED
ER...YEW ANY GOOD WIV THE KISSER LIFE ?

since der plunder did not up to der expectations come ve must advance to der enemy's hidden reserves
get at his personal possessions—his private account—his secret biscuit tin undt bottom drawer
YEA—KILROY—WE'RE WITH YOU TO A MAN
POSITIVELY
Q.172
GRRRR
BUT SPEAKIN' AS A CATERPILLAR AN' A BEETLE...
WE IS DECIDEDLY UNDECIDED

come oudt – come oudt du cowardly schweinhundts und help me face der enemy
SNUG INNIT ?
YEA – WHERE'S THE COCKTAIL CABINET ?
Q.173
HEY THERE – YOU, FELLOW
mit der strategic withdrawal
OI – WOT'S THIS ?
YEA, KILROY – GET OUT
THERE AIN'T EVEN ROOM ENOUGH FER US
KICK KICK

NOW FELLOW – EXPLAIN WHAT YOU'RE DOING ON MY PATCH
er... ulp... gulp
Q.174
AND WHERE ARE THOSE TWO KNAVES WITH WHOM I SAW YOU SKULKING ?
er... gasp... strangle
AND WOULD YOU MIND NOT SMOKING WHEN I'M TALKING TO YOU

I FIND SMOKING A STRANGE ENOUGH HABIT AT THE BEST OF TIMES—BUT BY YOUR MODE...
rauchen! verdammt schweinhunds
nicht rauchen nicht rauchen nicht rauchen ei'm sayink
CRIPES KILROY— WOT'RE YEW GOIN' ON ABOUT—WE AIN'T RAUCHENIN'
YEA—I'M JUST 'AVIN' A QUIET SMOKE
hilf
Q.175

hilf-hilf-fire-ei'm on fire
CRIPES—D'JEW 'EAR THAT?
YEA—THIS FLAMIN' THING'S OUTA CONTROL—'IT THE EMERGENCY EXITS
CRIPES—GOOD JOB THERE AIN'T ANY WOMEN OR CHILDREN ABOARD
YEA—THEY DO TEND TO GET UNDERFOOT IN AN EE-MER-JENSY
aa...
WAIT, KILROY, WAIT
—Y'GOT MY FAGS!
aaaagh
Q.176

THAT FLAMIN' TORTOISE 'AS 'AD IT AWAY WIV MY FAGS
TYPICAL, THAT IS — TYPICAL
Q.177
Y'CAN'T TRUST ANYBODY THESE DAYS (PRESENT COMPANY EXCEPTED)
YEA — AT LEAST WE GOT SOME INTEGRITY
OI — WOT'RE YOU DOIN' WIV YER 'AND IN MY POCKET ?
JUS' CHECKIN' ON HOW MUCH INTEGRITY YOU'RE CARRYIN'

YOO-HOO BOYS
Q.178
WHAT D'YOU THINK OF MY NEW HOLIDAY GEAR
IT'S THE 'FRONTIER' LOOK
IT'S WELL NAMED
WHERE'S THE NEAREST FRONTIER ?

YEA? WELL I S'POSE THAT'S THE SORT OF STUPID REACTION I SHOULD HAVE EXPECTED FROM YOU TWO CLOWNS
C'MON BABY GRUMPLIN' — WE'RE GOIN' HOME
Q.179
OH — OH — NOW IT'S COMIN' ON TO RAIN
BABY GRUMPLIN'? BABY ***GRUMPLIN'***?
LISTEN — WHEREVER YOU ARE
I'VE GOT ENOUGH GRIEF GOIN' ON WITHOUT YOU STARTIN'

CRIPES! LOOK GIRLS — HERE'S A SIGHT TO SEE
Q.180
CRUMBS — YEA! ***FOUR LEGS!***
OH... YEA — THAT TOO

... AN' I THOUGHT THE FLOUNCIN' OH-SO-FEMININE SKIRT, WITH A TOUCH OF FROU-FROU...
I FIND IT REMINISCENT OF THE COVERED WAGON
WELL, YES— IT DOES HAVE A CERTAIN EVOCATIVE...
ALL YOU NEED IS FOUR LARGE WHEELS
Q.181

I LIKE YOUR PEDAL-PUSHERS
OH... DO YOU ?
ALTHOUGH IT DOES SEEM AN OVER-AMBITIOUS TASK FOR LEGS LIKE YOURS
Q.182

MARLON — ARE YOU ALL PACKED FOR THE HOLIDAYS ?
YEA MAISIE — AN' I GOT THIS GREAT IDEA
— LIGHTEN THE LOAD SEE ? I GOT FED-UP WITH HUMPIN' THIS GREAT PACK YEAR AFTER YEAR
AN' WHAT'S **THAT** FOR ?
WELL I DON'T WANT TO FLOAT AWAY ALTOGETHER DO I ?
Q.183

OH MARLON — IT ***IS*** SWEET OF YOU TO CARRY THAT LITTLE BIT EXTRA FOR POOR, WEAK, HELPLESS ME
IT'S NOT THE TEENIEST BIT TOO HEAVY IS IT — EVEN FOR BIG, STRONG, EVER-SO-MANLY YOU ?
NO
IT'S JUS' THAT MY KNEES NEED THE EXERCISE
Q.184

I HOPE WE'RE NOT GOIN' TO END UP GETTIN' LOST AGAIN THIS YEAR
NO — THIS YEAR WE'RE GOIN' TO START OFF GETTIN' LOST
Q.185

AAGH
LOST— LOST—WE'RE LOST
LOST— MERCIFUL HEAVENS— LOST
LOST, AAGH, SOB, DOOM, LOST
CRUMBS MAISIE — WOT'S WRONG WITH YOU ?
Q.186

LISTEN, MAISIE, WE'RE NOT LOST—NOT WHILE WE'VE GOT OLE BOOT
DOGS HAVE GOT THIS SPECIAL INSTINC'
YEA— DOGS C'N FIND THEIR WAY OUT OF ANYTHIN'
HAVE I GOT NEWS FOR YOU
Q.187

BOOT! WHAT'RE YOU DOIN' IN THERE YOU GREAT HAIRY CLOWN?
Q.188
GRAB A LEG, SOMEBODY— WE'LL GIVE HIM A PULL
I'LL GET INSIDE AN' GIVE HIM A PUSH
WHADDA Y'MEAN— Y'CAN'T FIND Y'R WAY OUT?

LISTEN, MARLON, PUT Y'R LEFT LEG IN — Y'R RIGHT LEG OUT — Y'R LEFT LEG...
Q.189
NEVER *MIND* ABOUT THE HOKEY-COKEY!

LISTEN, MARLON — SLIDE Y'R FOOT IN — NO — NOT THAT FOOT — THE OTHER FOOT, NOW HOLD THE — NO, WAIT, BETTER HOLD THE...
OH I CAN'T STAND THIS — I CAN'T *STAND* IT
Q.190
AAAGH
WELL — THAT GOT RID OF THE WOODWORM

LISTEN, MARLON, JUST GET Y'R FEET IN AN' LET THEM DANGLE — HOLD ON TO THE TOP WITH Y'R HANDS
THAT'S IT — NOW **SLIDE**
Q.191
WOT NEXT?

MARLON'S DOWN THERE — UNDERNEATH THE **GROUND** — WHAT'RE WE GOIN' TO **DO** WELLIN'TON?
FRET NOT, MAISIE — WE'LL FORM A HUMAN CHAIN AN' **PULL** HIM OUT
Q.192
RIGHT — ALL TOGETHER 1-2-3- **HEAVE**
I DON'T WANT ANY **JOKES** — JUST HAND THEM BACK

LISTEN — WE'D BETTER GET OURSELVES TOGETHER AN' GET GOIN'
PRETTY SOON NOW NIGHT WILL FALL
AAAGH
WHY CAN'T IT JUS' COME DOWN GENTLY LIKE IT DOES BACK HOME ?
Q.193

THIS IS *ALL* WE NEEDED — *RAIN*
THIS TREE LEAKS
WHAT A ROTTEN TREE
COULDN' YOU HAVE PICKED A BETTER TREE ?
WHY DID YOU PICK THIS TREE ?
WELL IF *YOU* THINK *YOU* C'N PICK A *BETTER* ONE . . .
I'M NOT IN *CHARGE* OF *TREES*
Q.194

I'VE HAD ENOUGH OF THIS
I'M FED UP
AN' I'M GETTIN' FRIGHTENED
IT'S GETTIN' DARK
IF THERE'S ONE THING IN THE WORL' I CAN'T STAND IT'S THE DARK
Q.195
— AN' THUNDER
— AN' SHARKS
— AN' KING-KONG
DON'T BE RIDICULOUS MAISIE — YOU'RE NOT LIKELY TO SEE ANY SHARKS ROUN' HERE
— AN' EVEN LESS LIKELY TO SEE KING-KONG
— AN' IT'S NOT EVEN THUNDERIN'
KA-BOOM
I'LL LEAVE **YOU** TO DEAL WITH KING-KONG

CRUMBS WELLIN'TON — IS **KING-KONG** LIKELY TO BE COMIN' 'ROUN' 'ERE ?
— 'ES MY **FAVOURITE**
Q.196
IS **KING-KONG** LIKELY TO BE COMIN' 'ROUND HERE ?
MARLON — HE'S A **MODEL**
A **DUMMY**
IN A FILM MADE BEFORE YOU WERE EVEN **BORN**
AN' **YOU** ASK IF HE'S LIKELY TO BE COMIN' 'ROUND HERE ?
WELL — **IS** 'E OR **ISN'** 'E ?

I'M FED-UP WITH STUMBLIN' ABOUT IN THE DARK
Y'COULD ALWAYS TRY STANDIN' STILL
FOR A BLOKE WOT'S S'POSED T'BE INTELLIGENT YOU GET SOME PRETTY STUPID IDEAS
Q.197

WELLIN'TON — ARE WE GETTIN' ANYWHERE NEAR THERE ?
WE'RE ALMOST THERE —I C'N SMELL THE SEA
YOU'RE JUS' SAYIN' THAT TO ENCOURAGE US — I'LL BET
Q.198

WELLIN'TON — IS THIS YOUR IDEA OF A JOKE ?
NO
WELL WHAT'RE WE DOIN' HERE ? WHY DID YOU LEAD US INTO THE SEA ? YOU'VE GOT A LOT TO ANSWER FOR, WELLIN'TON — WHAT'S WRONG WITH YOU ? I DEMAND AN EXPLANATION AN' WHAT'S MORE . . .
WAIT, MAISIE, WAIT — I'VE CHANGED MY MIND
— THIS *IS* MY IDEA OF A JOKE
Q.199

THIS IS YOUR FAULT, WELLIN'TON, IT'S YOUR FAULT — YOU LED US UP TO OUR NECKS IN THE SEA — IT'S ALL YOUR FAULT
LEAVE OFF MAISIE — IT'S NOT MY FAULT — IT JUS' *HAPPENED* — IT'S NOBODY'S FAULT
I CAN'T STAN' THESE WEAK-KNEED EXCUSES
EVERYTHIN'S *SOMEBODY'S* FAULT
Q.200

WHAT'RE YOU MAKIN' BABY GRUMPLIN'?
a sand cottage
A SAND COTTAGE?
HOW QUAINT
SURELY YOU MEAN A SAND CASTLE
don't rub it in
i couldn't afford the mortgage
Q.201

maisie — would you like to buy my sand cottage?
NO THANK YOU, BABY GRUMPLING
you can have it for an ice-cream
I DO *NOT* WANT YOUR SAND COTTAGE AND I'M *NOT* GOIN' TO BUY YOU AN ICE-CREAM
oh what the hell
AAGH — STOPPIT - STOPPIT YOU LITTLE BEAST — ALL RIGHT — I'LL BUY YOU A ROTTEN ICE-CREAM
— there's more money in demolition
Q.202

COR — LOOK AT ALL THEM SEAGULLS — THERE MUS' BE **MILLIONS** OF'M — RIGHT ABOVE OUR HEADS
IT'S CONSIDERED INADVISABLE TO LOOK UP
OH... WHY
Y'MEAN — **EVERY** TIME I LOOK UP THEY'LL MESS ALL OVER MAISIE ?
Q.203

HULLO — WHERE'VE YOU TWO BEEN ?
I'VE BEEN SHOWING BABY GRUMPLIN' THE WONDERS OF THE SEA-SHORE
— WE FOUN' THIS CAVE — COR, TALK ABOUT ALADDIN'S CAVE
ALL THE **COLOURS** IN THE ROCKS — CRUSTED ALL OVER LIKE **JEWELS**, AN' DOWN IN THE **CRYSTAL-CLEAR ROCK POOLS...**
THE GENTLY SWAYIN' GORGEOUS SEAWEEDS AN' LITTLE WINKIN' ANENEMATHINGY'S IT WAS **FANTASTIC-MAGIC**—WASN' IT BABY GRUMPLIN' ?
i hurted mi toe !
Q.204

HOW DEEP D'YOU THINK IT IS HERE ?
Q.205
IT'S AS DEEP AS UP TO YOUR CHIN
YOU'RE RIGHT— CRUMBS —THEY THINK OF EVERYTHIN' ROUN' HERE
MIND YOU... WOT IF I'D ONLY WANTED IT AS DEEP AS UP TO MY CHEST ?

IT'S TIME FOR MY ANNUAL PEEP INTO THE ROCK-POOL TO QUIZ THE ANTICS OF THOSE CRANKY OLD CRABS
Q.206
...AND EVERY YEAR ABOUT THIS TIME THERE APPEARS THE EYEBALLS-IN-THE-SKY
A PHENOMENANA OF POOLIVERSAL STUPEFACTION WHICH
SOUNDS LIKE A LOAD OF OLD COD'S-WALLOP TO ME
DISBELIEVING DOLT — TREMBLE LEST VENGEANCE STRIKE YOU FROM...
ABOVE
I'M SURE IT'S ABOUT HERE SOMEWHERE
GAH
CRIPES — SO THAT'S WHAT VENGEANCE LOOKS LIKE
YEA — LOOKS LIKE IT'S STRUCK THE WRONG BLOKE
ANOTHER BOG-UP AT 'EAD OFFICE

Q.207
WOT'S GOIN' ON ?
WE'VE JUST SEEN VENGEANCE STRIKE
IS IT LIKE A LIGHTNING STRIKE ?
AAGH LISTEN YOU WITLESS WASTERS — THE SKY'S FALLING IN
REPENT — RECANT
OR A NUNOFFICIAL STRIKE
IT'S MORE LIKE A GREAT HAIRY FOOT STRIKE
OH — RIGHTO GUV
GLUG GLUG GLUG
WHAT'RE YOU DOING ? I SAID RECANT, NOT —
ROLL ME O-VER ROLL ME O-VER
OOOF
DON'T OOOF — HE SAID DON'T OOOF
I AIN'T OOOFED — 'AVE YOU ?
NAH — WE'VE JUST DECANTED LIKE 'E TOLD US
AN' DO IT AGAIN

Q.208
AWAY WITH OLD-FASHIONED, OUTDATED EYEBALLS-IN-THE-SKY
AAGH
SENSATION
EXCITATION
DOWN FROM THE SKY IT CAME — THE GREAT HAIRY
I BEAR WITNESS TO A NEW REV-ELATION
HEY—PSST—CYRIL—A WORD IN YOUR EAR
AGITATION
PERTURBATION
THE GREAT HAIRY WHAT ?
('OO'S GOT A STOCK OF 500,000 GLOW-IN-THE-DARK SOUVENIRS OF THE EYEBALLS-IN-THE-SKY ?)
WOT GREAT 'AIRY WOT ?
I KNOW NOT OF THE GREAT HAIRY WOT
WE HAVE
PRE-CISEMENTLY (AN' 'OO'S GOT ABSOLUTELY NO SOUVENIRS OF THE GREAT 'AIRY WHATEVER FROM WHEREVER ?)
ALL THAT'S KNOWN OF THE WOT IS — IT'S BIG AND HAIRY...
WE HAVE... OH... POINT TAKEN ALGERNON
— SO LET'S HAVE A GREAT COMEBACK WELCOME FOR THE GOOD OLD EYEBALLS-IN-THE-SKY
... BUT I DON'T THINK WE'RE GOING TO GET TO THE BOTTOM OF IT
I'D MUCH RATHER NOT — WHAT ?
— RAY
CHEERS
RAY

AND NOW BRETHREN – MY STOOGES – ER ASSISTANTS WILL PASS AMONG YOU WITH GENUINE APPROVED EYEBALLS-IN-THE-SKY SOUVENIRS
WHILE WE SING A FEW VERSES OF THE EYEBALLS-IN-THE-SKY ANTHEM
HOW MANY VERSES ARE THERE?
WELL THERE'S THE FIRST VERSE AFTER WHICH IT'S MUCH VERSE
THERE IS SOMETHING UP ON HIGH THAT LOOKS DOWN ON YOU AN' I...
SOUVENIRS – GET Y'R SOUVENIRS
–THE EYEBALLS – THE EYEBALLS-IN-THE-SKY
LOOK AT THIS – IT GLOWS IN THE DARK
I DON'T CARE IF IT SMOKES IN BED – TAKE IT AWAY
IT'S THE COSMIC PEEPIN' TOM AN' THERE'S NOWHERE TO HIDE FROM...
WOULD YOU LIKE A PHYLACTERY?
NO THANKS – I'LL STICK TO ALL-BRAN
–THE EYEBALLS – THE EYEBALLS-IN-THE-SKY
SO YOU CRABS BE-WARE OF THAT COSMIC STARE THERE ARE NAUGHTY THINGS YOU'D LIKE TO DO BUT YOU DON'T DARE...
WHAT'S THAT MOLE DOIN' HERE?
ISN' THIS ONE OF THE LYRICS MAURICE DODD WROTE?
AN' THAT SCRUTINISIN' GAZE HAS US LIVIN' IN A DAZE – THE EYEBALLS – THE EYEBALLS-IN-THE-SKY
YEA – WASN' IT A RECORD?
IT WAS MORE OF A DISASTER
Q.209

...AND NOW WE WAIT IN TREMBLING TREPIDATION
PSST – DO SOMETHIN' I THINK THEY'RE GETTIN' A LITTLE RESTLESS
WHERE'S THE NAFFIN' EYEBALLS?
SMASHYERFACIN
KICKYERUGLY
LETSAVEM OR YOU'LL GETTA BUNCHAFIVES
Q.210
SHOW THYSELF – ALL-POWERFUL ONE WHOSE VERY NAME STRIKES TERROR...
I DIDN'T KNOW THEY WERE EXPECTING ARTHUR SKARGILL
I KNOW THE ROCK-POOL'S ABOUT HERE SOMEWHERE
BY THE LORD HARRY – THESE ROCKS ARE SLIPPER–
EEEEE
AAGH
THE END IS NIGH
THEY WERE EXPECTING
IT'S AWFUL – TERRIFYIN'
I AGREE – NOT A PRETTY SIGHT
SHUTTUP – WE DON'T WANT A NASTY OUTBREAK OF SECONDARY PICKETIN'
HE WAS REFERRIN' TO THE JOKE

GLUTEUS MAXIMUS — MAY SHIPPAMS PRESERVE US!
HAIL — ALL HAIL — THE BEATIFIC BOTTOM
YOU SURE IT'S NOT THE GREAT 'AIRY WOT?
MAYBE THAT'S THE BOTTOM OF THE WOT TO WHICH WE NEVER GOT
Q.211
A FOOT — I CAN SEE A FOOT
I DO BELIEVE THAT'S THE ROCK-POOL I'VE BEEN LOOKING FOR
I'LL DIP IN FOR A DECKO
RETURN TO US — OH 'AIRY WOT
COME BACK OH BEATIFIC BOTTOM
SHOW THYSELF OH FULGENT FOOT
SAVED — SAVED BY THE EYEBALLS
IT'S BETTER THAN BEIN' RESCUED BY THE FUZZ
BOTTOM, WOT, FOOT & EYEBALLS
ISN' THAT THE NAME OF AN ADVERTISIN' AGENCY
YEA — THEY'VE GOT THE FIASCO ACCOUNT
I'M FEELIN' A BIT CONFUSED
I'M FEELIN' A CONFUSED BIT
EEK
ROOTY TOOTY
WHO IS THAT MOLE?

BEATIFIC BOTTOM
'AIRY WOT
FULGENT FOOT
AND NOW YOU EVIL BROTHERS AND SISTERS — THE EYEBALLS-IN-THE-SKY WILL BE WATCHING EVERY MOVE YOU MAKE
SNAP
CRACKLE
POP
WE'VE GOT A NICE LITTLE SCHISM GOIN' IN THIS CORNER
NOT GEORGE SCHISM — THE NOTED TROMBONERIST?
EEK — I'M MOVING TO THE NEXT FRAME
Q.212
— EVERY DIRTY DEED, POSTCARD, LAUNDRY
BUT MOST OF ALL THEY'LL BE WATCHING —
GET RIDDA THE EVIDENCE
THE VERY SAME
AAGH — IT'S EVEN WORSE IN THIS FRAME
HOW MUCH YOU'RE PUTTING IN THE COLLECTING-BOXES MY ACOLYTES ARE PASSING AMONGST YOU
CLINK
RUSTLE
CHINK
YOU DO, AN' YOU'LL GET A C.L.O.U.T.
I'M GIVING A MILLION
WE'D RATHER 'AVE THE MONEY
I'M GIVING MY NOTICE
I'M GIVING MY ALL
I'M GIVIN' A I.O.U.

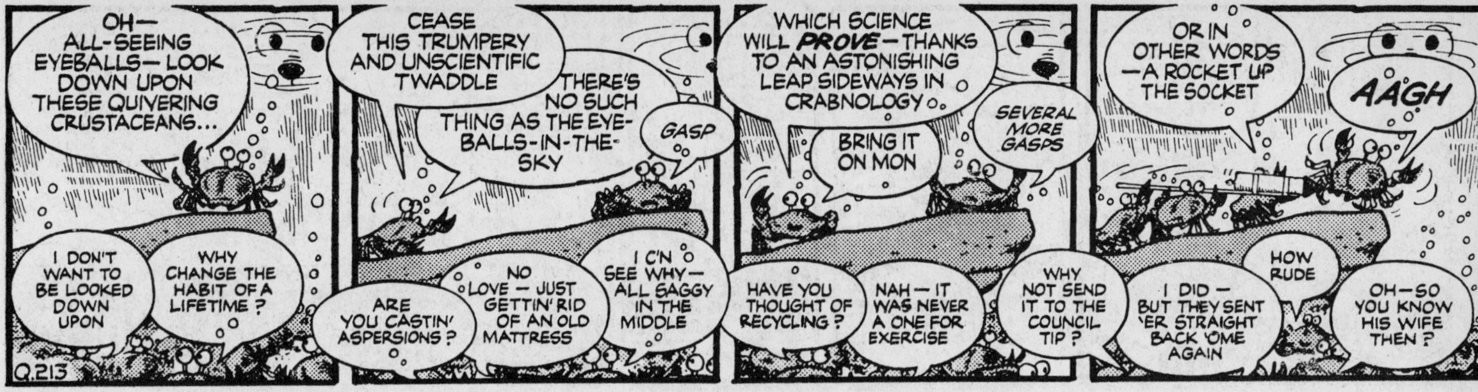
Q.213
OH— ALL-SEEING EYEBALLS— LOOK DOWN UPON THESE QUIVERING CRUSTACEANS...
I DON'T WANT TO BE LOOKED DOWN UPON
WHY CHANGE THE HABIT OF A LIFETIME ?
CEASE THIS TRUMPERY AND UNSCIENTIFIC TWADDLE
THERE'S NO SUCH THING AS THE EYE-BALLS-IN-THE-SKY
GASP
ARE YOU CASTIN' ASPERSIONS ?
NO LOVE — JUST GETTIN' RID OF AN OLD MATTRESS
I C'N SEE WHY— ALL SAGGY IN THE MIDDLE
WHICH SCIENCE WILL **PROVE**—THANKS TO AN ASTONISHING LEAP SIDEWAYS IN CRABNOLOGY
BRING IT ON MON
SEVERAL MORE GASPS
HAVE YOU THOUGHT OF RECYCLING ?
NAH — IT WAS NEVER A ONE FOR EXERCISE
OR IN OTHER WORDS —A ROCKET UP THE SOCKET
AAGH
WHY NOT SEND IT TO THE COUNCIL TIP ?
I DID — BUT THEY SENT 'ER STRAIGHT BACK 'OME AGAIN
HOW RUDE
OH—SO YOU KNOW HIS WIFE THEN ?

WITH THIS DEVICE WE'LL SOAR BEYOND THE CONFINES OF GRAVITY
YOU HAVE ABOUT YOU THE KNELL OF DOOM
WE'VE *ALL* BEEN ABOUT WITH NELLIE DOOM
I KNEW HER SISTER, LORNA
—AND EXPOSE THE MONSTROUS FALLACY OF THE EYEBALLS-IN-THE-SKY
DO NOT MEDDLE WITH MYSTERIES BEYOND YOUR KEN
EXPOSE THE *MONSTROUS FALLACY?*
SHRIEK
COME AWAY FROM 'ERE MILDRED
THERE'S ONE CRAB WHO CAN'T STAND THE VULGARITY
RUBBISH — IT'S NOT THE VULGARITY — IT'S THE COMPETITION
Q.214
RAISE THE INTERSTELLAR PROBE TO THE LAUNCH POSITION
READY WHEN YOU ARE Mr. DE-MILLE
AAGH — YOU'LL REND THE FABRIC OF THE POOLIVERSE
IF 'E GOES PROBIN' ROUND STELLA 'E'LL GET A NASTY SHOCK
SHE'S DEAD AGAINST SEXUAL HARASSMENT
I'M NOT TOO KEEN ON THAT HARRY SMENT MYSELF
HAVE A CARE— POLTROON
WHO *IS* THAT MOLE ?

Q.215
SPACE-PROBE READY FOR THE OFF, SPORT
FOOLS — YOU'VE GOT IT UPSIDE-DOWN
AAGH — SOMETHING'S GOING WRONG
DON'T PANIC — TRUST THE EXPERTS I ALWAYS SAY
WELL YOU KNOW WOT YOU ARE ...
UPSIDE DOWN? WHAT'S THAT POM PRATTLIN' ABOUT?
'E'S COMIN' THE RAW PRAWN — *THEY'RE* ALL UPSIDE DOWN — *WE'RE* THE RIGHT WAY UP
DID YOU CALL ME A GREAT 'AIRY WOT?
CLOSE — VERY CLOSE
AAGH — WE'RE ALL UPSIDE DOWN
S'FUNNY — HAVE YOU GOT VERTIGO?
ONLY TO THE NEXT FRAME
TOO TRUE, BLUE
FANCY A TUBA COLD FOSTERS?
WHY'RE THEY ALL ON THE CEILIN'?
GOOD ON YER, MATE
FLICKERIN' KNICKERS — WHAT'S GOIN' ON UP THERE?
WHO PUT THOSE AUSSIE CRABS IN CHARGE?
WHY DID I GET INTO THIS?
TURN OVER
TURN OVER
WHY'M I FEELIN' A BIT OF A FOOL?
THERE'S NOBODY INTELLIGENT AVAILABLE

Q.216
GET THOSE ANTIPODEAN BUFFOONS OUT OF IT — GET BACK ON YOUR FEET — AND GET THE SPACE-PROBE THE RIGHT WAY UP
SCUFFLE SHUFFLE
I DON'T KNOW IF I'M ON ME 'ARRIS OR ME ELBOW
WELL IF Y'R DRAWERS ARE HANGIN' *DOWN* *YOU'RE* THE RIGHT WAY *UP*
AN' VICE-VERSA
WHICH *IS* THE RIGHT WAY UP?
CRETINS — READ THE *INSTRUCTIONS*
MUTTER
MUTTER
WHAT'S ALL THIS VICE-VERSA STUFF?
TERRIBLE — EVEN THE POETS ARE BENT
GIVE ME A LONGFELLOW EVERY TIME
GIVE ME ANY FELLER — I'M NOT FUSSY
MUTTER
MUTTER
THERE'S A LOT OF MUTTERIN' GOIN' ON
DISGUSTIN' — WHY AIN'T I IN ON IT?
— HOW WILL YOU SPEND *YOUR* DAYS?
AT LAST I C'N GET ON WITH MY STAMP COLLECTION
OUCH — WHAT'S GOING ON?
I C'N GET ON WITH MY BUTTERFLY COLLECTION
I C'N GET ON WITH MY ELASTIC COLLECTION
EEK!
WELL IT SAID "*LIGHT BLUE PAPER AN' RETIRE*"
WE'RE LEAVIN' THE BLUE-PAPER BIT TO YOU

THE SCIENTIFIC EVENT OF THE CENTURY — RUINED — ABANDONED
LISTEN — I APPEAL TO YOU ALL
RUINED AN' ABANDONED — MY OWN STORY ENTIRELY
HERS IS A SAD END
AN' WRINKLED TOO
Q.217
I'M CALLING FOR VOLUNTEERS
AND IN PARTICULAR ONE LONE BRAVE VOLUNTEER
TO UNDERTAKE A MISSION OF DANGER, DISCOMFORT, HAZARD...
HEY — PSST
I'M VOLUNTEERING TO MAKE WAY FOR A VOLUNTEER
ME TOO
I DON'T LIKE THIS TALK OF UNDERTAKERS
NOR ME
NOR ME
WSP WSP WSP WSP WSP WSP WSP WSP WSP
— POINT TAKEN
— BY WHICH I MEAN THE JOB'S A DIABOLICAL FIDDLE — A PROPER DODDLE — A SKIVE — LOTSA DROPSY — TIME 'N'ARF — BIT ONNA SIDE — FREE...
— ONE VOLUNTEER I SAID — DAMMIT ONE VOLUNTAWK!
GEROUDOVIT I GOT PRIORITY
I GOT A UNION CARD
I GOT A RACE CARD
SINCE WHEN THEY BIN GIVIN' *THEM* OUT, MAN?

Q.218
RIGHT — ASSIST THE BRAVE VOLUNTEER TO THE SPACE-PROBE
I FEEL SICK
STICK A CORK IN HIS MOUTH
'RAY
CHEERS
OOH — ISN'T THIS EXCITING?
YES — BUT I WISH YOU'D LEAVE IT TILL LATER
RAISE IT TO THE LAUNCH POSITION
I WANNA GO TO THE LOO
— PASS ME ANOTHER CORK
FOOL — FOOL — STOP BEFORE IT'S TOO LATE
NO — I'VE ALWAYS BEEN BUILT THIS WAY
HULLO — IS THIS A NEW DEVELOPMENT?
AND SO CRABKIND TEARS ASIDE THE VEIL — SOARING THROUGH THE VERY CEILING OF THE POOLIVERSE
ER, GUV? GUV!
AAIEE
'RAY
— IT WON'T REACH
BOOO
A FIASCO
FAILURE
IT'S SHORT — IT'S FAR TOO SHORT
WHAT A MISERABLE PERFORMANCE
WHAT A LET-DOWN
"DEAR MARJ PROOPS..."

Q.219
IT'S NOT GOIN' TO WORK GUV —I CAN'T REACH
YOU RECKON WITHOUT THE RESOURCES OF HIGH CRAB-NOLOGY
OPERATE THE BOOSTER CATAPULT DEVICE
NOT MUCH ROOM FOR OUR BALLOONS IS THERE ?
NO
AAAGH
RIGHT
GO FORTH BOLD CRAB — FORTH INTO THE UNKNOWN WHERE NO CRAB HAS GONE BEFORE
JUST TRYIN' TO GET A WORD IN EDGEWAYS
WHAT'RE YOU DOIN' ?
—BUT DON'T OVERDO THE EXPENSES
YOU'LL NE-VER WALK A-LONE ♫

Q.220
AAAGH
IT'S 'ORRIBLE— 'ORRIBLE — I'VE JUST SEEN THE GREAT 'AIRY WOT
AN' IT 'ASN'T GOT A SHELL
NONSENSE — HOW CAN ANY-THING EXIST WITHOUT A SHELL —UNLESS IT'S A JELLY-FISH
THAT'S IT— SCIENCE HAS PROVED THE EYEBALLS-IN-THE-SKY IS REALLY NOTHING MORE THAN A MONSTROUS COSMIC JELLYFISH
YOU'RE A COSMIC BUFFOON SIR
I'M FEELIN' CONFUSED
I DIDN'T KNOW YOU COULD SEND 'IM BACK
THE RETURN OF THE GREAT 'AIRY WOT
YOU'N THE READERS BOTH
WHO IS THAT MOLE ?

WELL IF THOSE CRABS ARE STARTING TO LEAP OUT ON INNOCENT BYSTANDERS, I'M SLOPING OFF
Q.221
THE POOR BRAVE BOY'S OBVIOUSLY DELIRIOUS FROM HIS ORDEAL (HE'LL PROBABLY FALL OFF THE PODIUM ANY MINUTE NOW)
I TELL YOU I SAW THE GREAT 'AIRY WOT
THEY'VE GONE — YOU'VE OFFENDED THE EYEBALLS-IN-THE-SKY
YOU'VE DESTROYED THE FABRIC OF THE POOLIVERSE
TURNITIN
GETTOFF
THE EYEBALLS ARE NOTHING BUT A VAST COSMIC JELLY — PROBABLY THE UNIVERSAL JELLY FROM WHICH LIFE WAS FORMED
THAT'S IT! I'VE DISCOVERED THE SOURCE OF LIFE
AAAGH — I'M GOIN' TO 'AVE A NERVOUS BREAK-DOWN
I C'N GET IT FOR YOU WHOLESALE
THEY DON'T SEEM VERY PLEASED AT THE NEWS
BOO
GRRR
BUT IT WAS 'AIRY — I SAW IT — IT WAS 'AIRY
IT OBVIOUSLY HADN'T SHAVED THIS MORNING
DEATH AND PESTILENCE WILL SURELY FOLLOW
DEATH AND PESTILENCE? OH—A VERY NICE COUPLE
YEA — BUT THEY SHOULD NEVER'VE GONE IN FOR CATERING

Q.222
DOWN WITH TECHNOLOGICACKLE EXPLOITATION
I'M NOT WEARING ANY
DOWN WITH KNICKERS
TO THE BARRICADES
I'VE WARNED YOU ABOUT THAT BEFORE — CHIEF INSPECTOR
FOOL — YOU COULD'VE DESTROYED THE POOLIVERSE AND BROUGHT RUIN DOWN UPON US ALL
WELL — Y'CAN'T STOP PROGRESS
BACKS TO THE WALL MEN
KICK
CRIPES — THEY HAVEN'T GOT THE GAY LIB AS WELL?
GRR
SNAP
GOUGE
CLUMP
SHUTT'UP — WE'RE WITH ANYBODY
WE'RE WITH YOU COMRADES
'ERE — YOU SURE IT'S THEM WE'RE WITH?
HEAVE LUMPS OF COAL ATTEM — WE'RE TRYIN' TO RUN DOWN STOCKS
— IT'S KING ARTHUR AN' HIS NOT-ALL-THAT-MERRY-MEN
BLOW THIS — ONLY HALF-WAY THROUGH AND I'M KNACKERED ALREADY
NOW NOW DENNIS — HAVE A CUP OF TEA
BIFF
Merrymole the Magnificent
THAT'S WHAT THAT MOLE'S DOING — PLUGGING MAURICE DODD'S NEW BOOK
OI — GIT YORE FLICKERIN' TIARA OUTA MY LUG'OLE
STRUGGLE
MILDRED — I DON'T THINK THIS IS HARROD'S SUMMER SALE
IT'S BEEN CALLED THE MOST EXCITING WONDERFULLY SUPER-SPECIAL CHILDREN'S BOOK OF THE DECADE
WHO CALLED IT THAT?
— MAURICE DODD
WHERE WILL IT ALL END?
RIGHT HERE — THERE'S NO MORE ROOM

Q.223
HOW IS IT THE PURPOSE OF A JOURNEY SEEMS TO HAVE AN ALMOST TANGIBLE EFFECT ON THE DISTANCE TO BE TRAVELLED ?
THAT'S A NINTERESTIN' QUESTION, WELLIN'TON
YEA — OF RIVETIN' CONCERN TO A GIRL WITH BLISTERS — A BOOT FULL OF SWEAT AN' A KID BROTHER WHININ' TO BE CARRIED

Q.224
WELL HERE WE ARE THEN — BACK IN THE OLE ROUTINE
LATE BACK TO SCHOOL
WEEKS LATE BACK TO SCHOOL
WE C'N ALWAYS BLAME IT ON STRIKES — THERE'S BEEN LOTSANLOTSA STRIKES
RAIL STRIKES
SEA STRIKES
AIRPORT STRIKES
OH, YEA — I C'N JUS' SEE IT...
'...PLEASE MISS WE'RE LATE BECAUSE OF A-THREE-OUTDATED-PLATFORM-TICKETS-AN'-APPEALIN'-SMILES STRIKE'

WELL—HERE WE ARE, BOOT, HOME AGAIN
HOME, SWEET HOME, WHERE THERE'S NO PLACE LIKE —AN'...
Q.225
AN'...
I THINK I'LL GO OUT AN' START AGAIN

Q.226
RIGHT THEN—HOME FROM THE HOLS, TAKE TWO
W-E-L-L IT'S NOT ALL **THAT** BAD
ALL RIGHT— SO IT'S A BIT WORN AN' TORN
AN' IT'S STILL **HOME**
AN' EVEN IF THE GEAR **IS** A BIT OLD
—THERE'S A **BRAND NEW HOLE** IN THE FLOOR

IT'S STARTIN' ALREADY ISN' IT ?
THE GRIM DESCENT INTO EVERYDAY REALITY
NOW I'VE GOT A HOLE IN THE FLOOR
WHICH MEANS THE WHOLE BUILDIN'S ON THE VERGE OF SOMETHIN' OR THE OTHER
AN' I'VE GOT TO BEAR ALL THE RESPONSIBILITY
IT'S NOT FAIR
I'M ONLY A KID
WHAT'M I GOIN' TO DO?
IF ONLY YOU COULD DO SOMETHIN', BOOT
Q.227
LICK LICK LICK
— SOMETHIN' INVOLVIN' A HAMMER AN' NAILS IS MORE LIKE WHAT I HAD IN MIND

WELL — WHAT'RE WE GOIN' TO DO ABOUT IT ?
I KNOW— FOR THE TIME BEIN' LET'S STAN' SOMETHIN' OVER IT ... MAYBE COVER IT WITH A TABLECLOTH ... AN' A FEW FLOWERS
HEY WELLIN'TON —ALL SET FOR ...
— DID YOU KNOW YOU'VE GOT A HOLE IN YOUR FLOOR ?
Q.228
— I'M JUS' GOIN' TO PICK A FEW FLOWERS

ALL RIGHT WELLIN'TON — Y'VE 'AD YOUR LITTLE JOKE — NOW GET THIS LOT OFF ME
AN' GET ME OUTA THIS 'OLE
Q.229
HEY—HEY— I'M STUCK
DON' JUS' STAN' THERE — DO SOMETHIN'
LEMME SEE... SAUSAGES... EGGS.. CHIPS, (I KNOW YOU LIKE CHIPS, MARLON)... BACON (FANCY A BIT O'BACON, BOOT?)
WOT'RE Y'DOIN'— WOT'RE Y'DOIN'?
— I ASSUME YOUR MUM WILL SEND ROUN' MEALS?

NEVER MINE ABOUT MY MUM SENDIN' MEALS ROUN'— GET ME OUTA HERE!
Q.230
CRUMBS MARLON — YOU REALLY ARE STUCK
IT'S NO USE MARLON — WE CAN'T PULL YOU OUT
AN' I CAN'T HAVE YOU RUININ' MY DECOR BY STICKIN' UP IN THE MIDDLE OF THE ROOM LIKE THAT
LOOK — BEFORE WE START
SEE HOW MUCH FURTHER DOWN YOU CAN GET BY YOUR OWN UNAIDED EFFORTS

YOO-HOO WELLIN'TON— HAVE YOU SEEN MY MAR-
-LON
WHAT'S HE DOIN' DOWN THAT HOLE?
Q.231
HE'S STUCK, MAISIE — WE CAN'T PULL HIM OUT
STUCK? IMMOBILISED! UNABLE TO RESIST! OOH— HE'S GOIN' TO NEED CON-SO-LAY-SHUN
DON'T OO WORRY KISSY-FACE —IT'S MAISIE TO THE RESCUE
KISS KISS KISS
YEUK
— WITH ONE MIGHTY BOUND...

RIGHT... HAMMER... NAILS... PLANKS...
OH DO LEAVE OFF, BOOT
LICK LICK LICK
— NOW I'LL JUS' — CRUMBS GET OUT OF IT, BOOT
LICK LICK
LOOK —SHOVE OFF AN' FIND SOMETHIN' ELSE TO DO
NOW I'LL JUS' SEE IF...
AAAGH
LICK LICK LICK
Q.232
I'VE A FEELING THAT WASN'T WHAT HE HAD IN MIND

THERE'S SOMETHIN' HORRIBOBBLE DOWN THAT HOLE
BOOT
BOOT ?
Q233
TYPICAL THAT IS — NOW I REALLY NEED HIM
BOOT WHERE ARE YOU, BOOT ?
ROWF
THE NOBLE DOG RESPONDS TO THE CALL
AAAAGH
SOME DAYS THE NOBLE DOG CAN'T SEEM TO DO A DAM' THING RIGHT

AN' WHAT ARE YOU DOIN' MAY I ASK ?
Q.234
SKULKIN' WHILE I'VE BEEN FACIN' THE MORTAL DANGER OF THE-THING-IN-THE-HOLE
TWICE IT SNUCK UP ON ME
OH—I FOUGHT MIND YOU—FOUGHT LIKE A LION
BUT THE MEMORY WILL HAUNT ME FOREVER—A HORRIBLE, WET, SLOBBERY...
LICK LICK LICK
WILL YOU STOP THAT !

C'MON, BOOT, I WANT YOU TO GET DOWN AN' SEE WHAT'S IN THERE
BUT I KNOW WHAT'S IN THERE — ME
I CAN'T VERY WELL FIND ME IF I'M NOT THERE
AT LEAST I WAS
Q.235
THERE DOWN THERE — THAT'S WHERE YOU'RE S'POSED TO BE LOOKIN'
EVEN IF I WERE THERE I WOULDN'T GIVE MYSELF AWAY
WHAT'RE YOU DOIN'? WHAT'S GOIN' ON?
DEUCE TAKE IT — WHAT'M I GOING TO DO?
OH WELL — IT'LL HAVE TO BE THE OLD STANDBY
SOMETIMES I THINK DOGS ARE STUPID
ARF ARF ARF
SOMETIMES IT'S THE ONLY WAY TO BE

LISTEN, BOOT, IT'S NOT OFTEN YOU'RE ASKED TO EARN YOUR KEEP
BUT THERE'S SOMETHIN' HORRIBOBBLE DOWN THERE AN' I WANT YOU TO DO SOMETHIN'
OH WELL — I SUPPOSE I'D BETTER PUT ON A PERFORMANCE
WROWF WROWF
AAGH — WE DON'T WANT THAT LOT ALL OVER THE HOUSE
QUICK — RUSH ROUN' AN' BARK 'EM ALL BACK IN AGAIN
Q.236

Q.237
RIGHT BOOT— DO A WIDE SWEEP AN' HERD ALL THOSE CRAWLIES BACK DOWN THAT HOLE
I'LL GET SOME MORE WOOD AN' EXTRA LONG NAILS
WROWF
WROWF WROWF
I THOUGHT I HAD SOME IN HERE... OR WAS IT THE TEA-CADDY ?
GRRR
WROWF
RIGHT— MOVE TO ONE SIDE AN' I'LL...
WHAT'S THE BETTIN' YOU'RE EXPECTIN' ME TO SAY— "THERE'S A CLEVER DOG"

THAT'S *THAT*
THEM NAIL-POINTS ARE PROBABLY CAUSIN' A PROBLEM SOMEWHERE IN AUSTRALIA
—PUSH THE OLE ARMCHAIR ON TOP OF IT
THE ONLY THING IS —THAT HORRIBOBBLE WET SLOBBERY THING WHICH REACHED *OUT* OF THE HOLE
IS THAT NOW *INSIDE* THE HOLE OR...?
Q.238

SWEET LASS OF RICHMOND HILL— SWEET LASS OF...
—WILL I DO INSTEAD, SAILOR ?
ZOUNDS— 'TIS TATTY OLDBITT (THE SAILORS' FRIEND)
'OW ABOUT A BIT OF A WELCOME 'OME—I'VE BIN TO THE FORKLAN'S
BY THE LORD HARRY— MIXED UP IN THAT ARGIE-BARGY WERE YOU ?
I WENT TO GIVE SOUTHERN—I MEAN—SUCCOUR AN' COMFORT TO THE BOYS IN (WHOOPS) BLUE
—WERE YOU SECONDED BY THE NAVY ?
—NO—MOSTLY I WAS THIRDED AN' FOURTHDED
—SOME O'THEM EVEN SAID THEY'D RATHER 'ANG ON TILL THEY GOT BACK 'OME
Q.239

LISSEN SAILOR—IT'S BIN A LONG AN' WEARY VOYAGE BACK 'OME —GIVE US A KISS
OOH (HIC) YOU'VE TURNED THE LIGHT ORF YOU NAUGHTY BOY
Q.240
—THERE'S NO NEED TO WIV ME, DEARIE, I'M NOT SHY AN' (WHOOPS)
I KNOW THINGS WERE ROUGH IN THE FALKLANDS, TATTY, BUT YOU DO SEEM A LITTLE MORE-THAN-WORSE-FOR-WEAR
I'M NOT SURPRISED—I ENDED UP WITH A PRETTY WILD AN WOOLLY BUNCH
OH... A BIT LIBERAL AND FOUL-MOUTHED WERE THEY ?
—WE NEVER DIS-CUSSED (HIC) POLITICS
AS FOR FOWL-MOUTHED —FAR FROM IT— ALL THEY EVER SAID WAS B-A-A-A
YOU'VE TURNED THE LIGHT ON AGAIN I SEE—CHEEKY

DID YOU SEE ANYTHING OF THE ARGENTINES WHILE IN THE FALKLANDS, TATTY ?
WHY'RE YOU (HIC) UPSIDE-DOWN
OH—ALL THE TIME, SAILOR, ALL THE TIME
'ERE — YOU'VE TURNED THE LIGHT OFF AGAIN
THERE I WAS WIV THE NAVY — THEY SENT ME TO THE ARGIES — BACK I WENT TO THE NAVY
OH — YOU WERE A PLENIPOTENTIARY ?
AS FAR AS I WAS CONCERNED THERE WAS PLENNY O' NOTHIN'— WHERE ARE YOU ?
NO — NO — I MEAN YOU WERE BEING USED AS A GO-BETWEEN
WELL — NO — I FOUND OUT I WAS BEIN' USED AS A THREAT
I DO WISH YOU'D STOP MESSIN' ABOUT WIV THE LIGHTS AN' START MESSIN' ABOUT WIV ME
Q.241

OI SAILOR— YOU'RE GOIN' IN THE WRONG DIRECTION— I'M OVER 'ERE
FIRST OF ALL 'E'S MESSIN' ABOUT WIV THE LIGHTS AN' NOW 'E WANTS A BIT OF (HIC) KISH-CHASHE
C'MON DEARIE — GIVE A GIRL A GRAPPLE
ER— FIRST A FEW MORE OF YOUR FASCINATING FALKLANDS STORIES— DID YOU SEE MUCH NAVAL ACTION ?
—'ARDLY ANY
THEY WAS ALL TOO BUSY RUNNIN' ABOUT FIRIN' GUNS AN' STUFF
'ERE — YOU DON'T WANNA TIRE YOURSELF OUT — YOU'LL BE IN THE SAME STATE AS THEM FLAMIN' GUNNERS
Q.242

RIGHT DEARIE — NOW YOU'VE 'AD YOUR WORK-OUT P'RAPS WE C'N GET DOWN TO SOME ACTION OF OUR OWN
PANT PANT
LISTEN, TATTY, LISTEN
WHEN I ASKED IF YOU'D SEEN ANY NAVAL ACTION I WAS REFERRIN' TO AN ON-DECK RÔLE
OOH — ME TOO — THERE'S NOTHIN' LIKE A ROLL ON THE DECK IN A GOOD 'EAVIN' SEA — IT BEATS — 'ERE — WHERE YOU GOIN'?
Q.243

LOOK, SAILOR — I'M ALL FOR A BIT OF PRELIMINARY LARKIN' ABOUT MYSELF BUT...
DEY-VIL TAKE IT MADAM — ARE YOU INSATIABLE ?
YOU'VE JUST FINISHED TELLING ME YOU WERE IMPORTUNING THE SAILORS E'EN WHILST THEY WERE AT ACTION STATIONS
WELL AS I SAID TO THE ADMIRAL — ALL WORK AN' NO PLAY MAKES JACK COME OVER A BIT PECULIAR — SO I VOLUNTEER...
NEXT THING I KNEW I WAS BEIN' CATAPULTED AT THE ENEMY
— WE'D RUN OUT OF AMMO — GISH A KISH (HIC)
Q.244

YOU BEAST — YOU'RE DRAGGIN' ME DOWN TO YOUR LEVEL — I'M VERY PLEASED TO SAY
— WHAT WAS THE POINT OF LAUNCHING **YOU** AT THE ARGENTINES TATTY OLDBITT?
I WAS A PIECE OFFERIN' — THOUGH NOBODY SAID WHAT PIECE I WAS TO OFFER A NOD'S AS GOOD AS...
YOU MEAN YOU WERE OFFERING ***TERMS?***
OH YERSE — THE USUAL TERMS
WELL WHY NOT? THEY WERE ONLY MEN — LONELY AN' LONGIN' FOR...
BUT ENOUGH OF THIS CHAT — LET'S LIVE FOR TODAY
WAIT WAIT— WHAT WAS THEIR REACTION?
THEY RAN UP A WHITE FLAG
THEY ALSO RAN UP LADDERS, SIDE STREETS, LAMP-POSTS — I'M BEGINNIN' TO THINK IT'S CATCHIN'
Q.245

DESERTED, ABANDONED, CAST ASIDE LIKE A BROKEN TOY
OH — IT'S AN OLE OLE TALE — IT'S ALWAYS THE WOMAN WOT PAYS
WELL — IF SHE'S ON LARGE G.&T.'s SHE DOES
MEN'VE BIN MY (HIC) RUIN
NO, WAIT (WHOOPS) **DRINK** 'AS BIN MY RUIN
ALL RI' THEN MEN ***AN'*** DRINK 'AVE BIN MY RUIN
WELL GIVIN' UP DRINK IS NO PROBLEM — SEEIN' AS 'OW I'M SKINT
WOT WORRIES ME IS ...
WOT'M I GOIN' TO DO WHEN I LOSE MY ***LOOKS?***
Q.246

YOU KNOW WHAT, BOOT, I'VE BEEN THINKIN'
YOU KNOW NEX' MONDAY'S MY BIRTHDAY — AN' DAY OF NASHNUL REJOICIN' (OCT. 25th — FOR THOSE WHO WANT TO TAKE NOTES)
WELL I'D LIKE A RECORD PLAYED ON THE RADIO ON MY BIRTHDAY
SO I'M GOIN' TO WRITE TO A D.J.
IN FAC' — TO MAKE SURE I'LL WRITE TO ALL OF 'EM
MIND YOU — I S'POSE I'LL HAVE TO KID 'EM ALONG A BIT
— ASSURE EACH AN' EVERY ONE I'M A REGULAR LISTENER TO THEIR PROGRAMME
WELL THAT'S NOT TOO DIFFICULT
RIGHT — EYES DOWN ...
'GLORIOUS HONEYBUN — DEAR SIR ...'
Q.247

IF I C'N KID ALL THESE D.J.'s I'M A REGULAR LISTENER, ONE O'THEM'S BOUND TO PLAY A REQUEST ON MY BIRTHDAY
— OCT. 25th.
"DEAR TERRY WOGAN OR, AS YOU'RE AFFECTIONATELY KNOWN IN THIS HOUSEHOLD — TAFFY ..."
"DEAR JIMMY YOUNG — HAVIN' ENJOYED MANY A GLASS OF YOUR EXCELLENT TARTAN BITTER ..."
"DEAR KENNY EVERETT — AS A REGULAR LISTENER TO YOUR RELIGIOUS AFFAIRS PROGRAMME"
CRUMBS, BOOT, THIS IS PRETTY HARD WORK
I DO HOPE I'M NOT WASTIN' MY TIME
Q.248

"DEAR JIMMY SAVILE —I REGULARLY USE YOUR FIXIT FOR MY DENTURES..."
ONE O'THESE D.J.'s IS BOUND TO PLAY A REQUEST ON MY BIRTHDAY, BOOT
"DEAR DAVE-LEE-TRANSVERSE —HOW CLEVER OF YOU TO INVENT SIDEWAYS RADIO AN'..."
"DEAR ENOCH POWELL..."
—NO WAIT
I MIGHT HAVE GOT THAT WRONG
IS IT ENOCH ?
HE'S A POLITICIAN OR SOMETHIN' ISN' HE ?
OH WELL— I WOULDN' SNIFF AT A STATEMENT IN THE HOUSE
Q.249

Q.250
"DEAR DAVID JENSEN, I'M CONSIDERIN' PURCHASIN' ONE OF YOUR CARS AN'..."
WOT'RE YOU DOIN' WELLIN'TON ?
OH—H'LO MARLON
I'M WRITIN' TO ALL THE D.J.'s—ASKIN' THEM TO PLAY A REQUEST ON MY BIRTHDAY
MIND YOU —I'M HAVIN' TO BUTTER THEM UP A BIT
—PRETEND I'M A REGULAR LISTENER TO THEIR PROGRAMMES AN' SUCH
YEA BUT IF YOU'RE NOT— YOU'RE CHEATIN' —GROSS MISREPHEN-SIBILISATION ... AN' THAT
MISREPRE-SENTATION ? IS THAT WHAT YOU'RE ACCUSIN' ME OF ? HOW NAÏVE CAN YOU GET ?
THEY'RE ALL AT IT
I'LL BET THAT THERE TONY BLACKTHORNE DOESN' EVEN DRINK HIS OWN CIDER

Q.251
"DEAR MICHAEL ASPEL —AS A REGULAR VISITOR TO YOUR ZOO..."
THE CHEEK OF THAT MARLON—SAYIN' I WAS CHEATIN'
I CAN'T LISTEN TO EVERY PROGRAMME CAN I ?
ANYWAY— I DON'T EVEN KNOW IF ALL THESE PEOPLE ARE REAL
I MEAN — THEY'RE ONLY VOICES— I'VE NEVER SEEN THEM
FOR ALL I KNOW THEY COULD ALL BE THAT MIKE YAHOO THROWIN' HIS VOICE

"DEAR ED STEWPOT—HOW CLEVER OF YOU TO INVENT THOSE SUPER SNACKS WHAT YOU POUR HOT WATER ON AN'..."
OH...I DUNNO...
MAYBE I AM CHEATIN'— LYIN' EVEN
Q.252
MAYBE I SHOULD ADMIT TO THESE D.J.'s I DON'T LISTEN TO ALL THEIR PROGRAMMES—BUT ASK THEM TO PLAY A REQUEST ANYWAY
"DEAR MIKE READ, SIMON BATES, DAVID HAMILTON, PETER POWELL, TONY PRINCE, BRIAN MATHEWS...
WOULD YOU PLAY A RECORD FOR ME ALTHOUGH I'M NOT A REGULAR LISTENER
LICK LICK
—ALTHOUGH I WOULD BE IF I COULD
IT'S ONLY BECAUSE OF MY WICKED STEPMOTHER WHO TAKES MY RADIO AWAY AN' LOCKS ME UP IN A DUNGEON WITHOUT FOOD OR WATER AN'..."
BELIEVE ME I WOULD

ISN' IT EXCITIN'?
MURMUR
D'YOU THINK THERE'LL BE REFRESH-MENTS?
D'YOU REALLY THINK THEY'LL PLAY A SPECIAL REQUEST?
I'M SITTIN' ON SOMETHIN' NASTY
WE'RE ALL SITTIN' ON SOMETHIN' NASTY
BUZZ
MURMUR
THEY'RE BOUND TO
MAYBE EVEN A QUEEN'S SPEECH
ALTHOUGH I DID LEAVE IT A BIT LATE BEFORE DROPPIN' HER MAJESTY A NOTE
—AND THIS IS SAM COSTA WITH A SPECIAL REQUEST FOR...
'E SAID IT WAS GOIN' TO BE TERRY WOBURN
OR EVEN KENNY EVEREST
IF YOU ASK ME 'ES POTTY THAT KID
AN' WOT'S MORE NOT EVEN A BAG OF CRISPS
MUTTER GROAN
GRR
HOW HUMIL-ERATIN'—AN' I ASKED ALL MY INFERENTIAL SCHOOL-FRIENDS ROUN'
WELL—LOOK—IT IS A VERY OLD RADIO
I'M GONNA GET LIT UP WHEN THE LIGHTS GO WHOOOEEE SCREEK SCREEK
LICK LICK
Q.253

WHAT'RE YOU DOIN' MARLON?
WORKIN' ON MY NEW PROJEC'—PLANS FOR THE CHANNEL TUNNEL
THE CHANNEL TUNNEL? ER...YOU KNOW SEVERAL PEOPLE HAVE ALREADY HAD A GO AT THAT
YEA—AN' THE GUVMINT KEEPS STOPPIN' THEM
—BEIN' AFRAID OF ALL THEM FRENCHIES FLOODIN' THROUGH THE TUNNEL WIVOUT PAYIN' DUTY ON THEIR ONIONS—I KNOW ALL THAT
BUT WIV MY PLAN THE GUVMINT WON'T KNOW IT'S GOIN' ON
OH? HOW'S THAT GOIN' TO BE MANAGED?
—BY WORKIN' AT NIGHT
Q.254

BUILDING THE CHANNEL TUNNEL
1 You will need:
'OW DO
BON JAW
1 ENGLISHMAN
1 FRENCHMAN
(OR LARGE LADIES MITE DO)
2 SHUVELLS
1 SMALL PILOT HOLE
1 WIDE HOLE
DIAGRAM A Note: THIS IS NOT TO SCAIL
ENGLAND
Old Fashiond moad of transport
FRANCE
BORE A SMALL PILOT HOLE
B
OUR DAYS ARE NUMBERD
KEEP DIGGING ALL ROUND PILOT HOLE– FROM EACH END
C
Q.255
MARK MI WERDS —NO GOOD WILL CUM OF IT
OOPS
SACRED BLUE
UNTIL YOU MEAT IN THE MIDDEL
(GRATE CARE IS NEEDED AT THIS POINT)

I'M NOT ONE TO DISCOURAGE VISION AND INITIATIVE BUT THERE REALLY ARE A FEW PROBLEMS INHERENT IN YOUR CHANNEL TUNNEL SCHEME, MARLON
WOT ?
WELL– FOR A START –LOOK AT THE ANGLE YOU'RE PROPOSIN'
A CAR OR LORRY USIN' THAT WOULD DROP STRAIGHT ON ITS NOSE
OUCH!
Q.256
THE INVENTIVE BRANE IS AT ITS BEST WHEN FACED WITH A CHALLENGE, WELLINTON
I'VE JUST FOUND A NEW USE FOR OLD MATTRESSES
–THE KIND OF THINKIN' WOT MADE THIS COUNTRY GRATE
MAGNY-FEEK, THIS EST JUST LE JOB
CUSHON EFFECT

Q.257
YOU PLAN TO START YOUR CHANNEL TUNNEL WITH A SMALL PILOT HOLE ?
S'RIGHT
SMALL PILOT HOLE
—AN' THEN DIG ALL ROUN' IT TO MAKE THE BIG TUNNEL HOLE ?
RIGHT AGAIN
—WELL HOW'RE YOU GOIN' TO MAKE THE SMALL PILOT HOLE IN THE FIRST PLACE ?
ER...
?
...WIV A SMALL PILOT ?

I DON'T THINK DROPPIN' A SMALL PILOT ON HIS HEAD IS GOIN' TO PROVIDE A SMALL PILOT HOLE FOR YOUR CHANNEL TUNNEL SCHEME, MARLON
OH? WHY NOT?
WELL— EVEN THE SMALLEST PILOTS ARE NOT KNOWN FOR HAVIN' HARD POINTED HEADS WITH ROCK-DRILLIN' PROPERTIES
CRIPES—A REPRIEVE
—S'POSE WE PERVIDED 'IM WIV A NARD POINTED 'AT ?
AAGH
EVEN SO HOW WILL HE KNOW WHICH WAY TO GO AFTER IMPACT ?
WELL... S'POSE WE FIRST MADE A NEXTRA SMALL PILOT HOLE FOR THE SMALL PILOT HOLE ? (Diagram Ⓐ)
A
B
—THE ONLY WAY OUT (Diagram Ⓑ)
Q.258
IT WAS ONLY A SUGGESTION

HEY—WELLIN'TON— I'VE SOLVED THE PROBLEM OF 'OW TO DIG THE SMALL PILOT 'OLE FOR MY CHANNEL TUNNEL SCHEME
REALLY MARLON? (SIGH) I'M ALL AGOG
YEA—LOOK —WIV A 'IGHLY TRAINED MOLE (Diagram Ⓐ)
A
DIPLOMA
NO WAY
MARLON...HOW D'YOU THINK YOU'RE GOIN' TO PERSUADE A MOLE TO DIG ALL THE WAY FROM ENGLAND TO FRANCE
Q.259
—PERVIDE A NINCENTIVE (Diagram Ⓑ)
YOIKS— LA CRUMPET FRANÇAISE
COOEE— VOUS KNOTTY BOY VOUS
B

OK MARLON— HAVIN' GOT A (SIGH) MOLE TO DIG YOUR CHANNEL TUNNEL PILOT-HOLE—WHAT'S THE NEXT STEP?
OOO-LA-LA WALKEZ-VOUS THIS WAY, DEARIE
WHOOPEE
C
BREAKTHREW ACHEAVED BY HIGHLY MOTIVATED MOLE
—FOR THE BIGGER HOLE WE BRING ON A BIGGER MOLE (Diagram Ⓓ)
D
BIGGER MOLE
REALLY? IT'LL HAVE TO BE A (HEE-HEE) CONSIDERABLY BIGGER MOLE
YEA—WELL— COURSE I MEANT A CONSIDERABABLY BIGGER MOLE (Diagram Ⓔ)
?
E
CONSIDERBADABL
LOTS BIGGER MOLE
—IN FAC' IT'D HAVE TO BE GINORMOUS
YEA—WELL— IT'S ALL A MATTER OF PROPORTION INNIT? (Diagram Ⓕ)
F
NELSONS COLLUM
Q.260

APART FROM THE RIDICULOSITY OF USIN' A **MOLE** TO DIG THE **CHANNEL TUNNEL** — YOU'RE PROPOSIN' A MOLE OVER **TWICE** THE SIZE OF NELSON'S COLUMN
RIGHT — WELL E'S GOT T'BE **BIG** 'AS'N 'E ?
Q.261
BUT LOOK'T THE SIZE OF HIM — HE MUST WEIGH, LEMME SEE ... ABOUT 5,000,000 TONS
YEA — JUS' ABOUT WOT I CALCU-WOTSITED 5,000,000 TONS
BUT THINK OF THE **WEIGHT** — IT'D GO THROUGH THE EARTH'S **CRUST**
OH WELL — I'VE GIVEN UP THE CHANNEL TUNNEL
GOOD
I GOT **ANOTHER** IDEA
BUILDING THE AUSTRALIA TUNNEL
YOU WILL NEED: A 5,000,000 TON MOLE

... AN' ENDIN' UP WITH A 5,000,000 TON (*HEE HEE HEE*) MOLE
OH IT'S ALL VERY WELL FOR YOU TO CRITI-SAYS, WELLIN'TON
— BUT AT LEAST MAY MAWLON'S GOT **PLANS**
DRAIVE
EMBITION
WHAT DO **YOU** EVER DO? TELL ME **ANYTHIN'** YOU EVER DO
WELL I ... THAT IS ... WELL Y'JUS' CAN'T ... AN' ANYWAY ...
PREE-SAYSLEY
... AFTER ALL, *MUMBLE MUMBLE*, AN' WHAT'S MORE, *MUMBLE MUMBLE*
... ON TOP OF WHICH, *MUMBLE MUMBLE*, FLAMIN' CHEEK *MUMBLE MUMBLE* ...
— AN' COME TO THAT — WHAT DO **YOU** DO, 'CEPT LOAF AROUN' ALL DAY
Q.262

I'VE JUS' BEEN TALKIN' TO WELLIN'TON — YOUR SO-CALLED BES' FRIEN'
— TAKIN' THE MICKEY HE WAS, MARLON — LAUGHIN' AT YOUR PLANS FOR THE CHANNEL TUNNEL
OH I **TOLD** HIM I DID — SAID YOU WERE BRIGHTER THAN WHAT **HE** WAS — AN' ***INTELLIGENT* — *WIDE-AWAKE* — *AMBITIOUS***
Q.263
O'COURSE — I WAS MAKIN' IT ALL UP

Y'KNOW BOOT— MAYBE MAISIE WAS ***RIGHT*** ABOUT ME NOT REALLY ***DOIN'*** ANYTHIN'
I MEAN — WHAT ***DO*** I DO ?
— GET UP, GO TO SCHOOL, PLAY ABOUT A BIT...
... MAYBE DO A BIT OF READIN'
BEFORE Y'KNOW IT I'M BACK IN BED AGAIN
I MEAN — I'M NOT REALLY ***GETTIN'*** ANYWHERE
(SIGH) I SOMETIMES GET THE FEELIN' LIFE IS PASSIN' ME BY
Q.264
— I ALSO GET THE FEELIN' MY SUPPER IS AS WELL

SAUSAGE STEALER
COME BACK — COME BACK —YOU ROTTEN TEALEAF—I'LL —OH
OH, BOOT, I'VE JUST NOTICED— YOUR BOWL'S EMPTY
OH DEAR, OLE FRIEN', I HAVEN'T FED YOU TODAY
OH BOOT—I'M FILLED WITH REMORSE
NEVER MIND—I'M FILLED WITH SAUSAGES
Q.265

BOOT—I'M SORRY I FORGOT TO FEED YOU
—TELL YOU WHAT—WE'LL SHARE
THOSE SAUSAGES
YOU TOOK
WHERE ARE THEY?
YOU'VE EATEN THEM, HAVEN'T YOU— YOU'VE EATEN THEM!
BY THE LORD HARRY—THE RAPIDITY WITH WHICH HE CRAWLED TO THAT CONCLUSION
NO WONDER THEY HAD TO INVENT COMPUTERS TO DO THEIR THINKING FOR THEM
Q.266

I'M ASTONISHED, SADDENED AN' DISGUSTED
SOUNDS LIKE A FIRM OF SOLICITORS
WHAT-EVER HAPPENED TO FRIENDSHIP, LOYALTY AN' TRUST
WITH NAMES LIKE THAT THEY PROBABLY WENT OUT OF BUSINESS
Q.267
HOW COULD YOU DO IT—HOW COULD YOU BE SO MEAN—SO GREEDY?
BY THE LORD HARRY—WHAT IS THE LITTLE FELLOW TALKING ABOUT
—EATIN' ALL THE SAUSAGES—A WHOLE POUND OF SAUSAGES
WHAT? BUT THAT WAS HALF AN HOUR AGO
—TALK ABOUT HARBOURING A GRUDGE

HERE I GO —SUPPERLESS TO BED
AN' WHY?
'COS YOU ATE ALL THE SAUSAGES
AT LEAST I GO WITH A CLEAR CONSCIENCE—WHILE YOU'RE FILLED WITH GUILT
IF IT CAN FIND ROOM AMONGST THE SAUSAGES
Q.268
REMEMBER THIS—VIRTUE IS ITS OWN REWARD
—IT HAS THE ADDED ADVANTAGE OF BEING VERY LOW IN CALORIES

Q.269
MORNIN' BOOT — LOOKS LIKE BEIN' A NICE . . . OH — I FORGOT
— I'M NOT TALKIN' TO YOU
ON ACCOUNT OF YOU PINCHED ALL THE SAUSAGES LAS' NIGHT
HE'S GOT A MEMORY LIKE AN ELEPHANT THIS LAD
WHAT A PITY THE REST OF HIM ISN'T BUILT TO MATCH

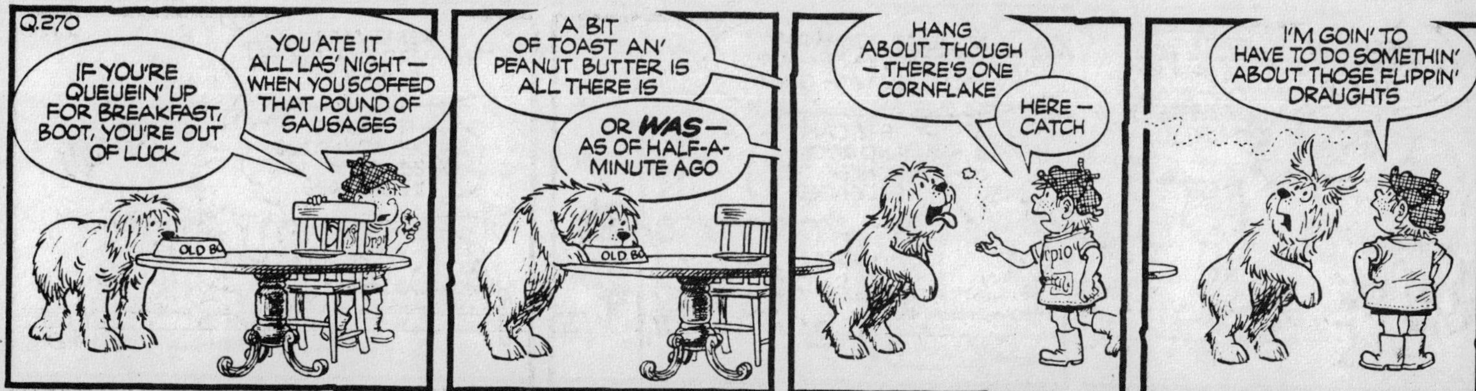
Q.270
IF YOU'RE QUEUEIN' UP FOR BREAKFAST, BOOT, YOU'RE OUT OF LUCK
YOU ATE IT ALL LAS' NIGHT — WHEN YOU SCOFFED THAT POUND OF SAUSAGES
A BIT OF TOAST AN' PEANUT BUTTER IS ALL THERE IS
OR WAS — AS OF HALF-A-MINUTE AGO
HANG ABOUT THOUGH — THERE'S ONE CORNFLAKE
HERE — CATCH
I'M GOIN' TO HAVE TO DO SOMETHIN' ABOUT THOSE FLIPPIN' DRAUGHTS

BOOT — IT'S NO USE YOU FOLLOWIN' ME ABOUT
THERE'S NOTHIN' TO EAT 'TIL I C'N GET FRESH SUPPLIES
AN' I'VE GOT TO GO TO SCHOOL NOW
ANYWAY — A BIG DOG LIKE YOU SHOULD SHOW SOME INGENUITY
WHY DON'T YOU GO OUT AN' GET A RABBIT ?
GET A **RABBIT ?** WHAT MANNER OF DAM' FOOL SUGGESTION IS THAT ?
BREAKFAST IS THE BURNING ISSUE OF THE MOMENT
THIS IS **NO TIME** FOR MESSING ABOUT WITH **CONJURING TRICKS**
Q.271

I SAY THERE — YOU THERE — FELLOW
HOW'D YOU LIKE TO BECOME PART OF MY CORPORATE IDENTITY — IN A, *HA-HUM,* **CULINARY** CAPACITY
— AN **INSIDE** JOB, WHAT ? *HA-HA,* FILL FULL — I MEAN **FULFILLING** AN ABSOLUTELY **VITAL** RÔLE
FILLING A **VACANT** POSITION
YOU'LL BE **COMPLETELY ABSORBED** INTO THE ORGANI.... *(OH, DEYVIL TAKE IT)*
— IT'S **TOO MUCH** WHEN YOUR PROSPECTIVE LUNCH SITS UP AND WIGGLES ITS NOSE AT YOU
Q.272

Q.273
AHA!
WELL I'VE CERTAINLY NO COMPUNCTION ABOUT PUTTING YOU ON MY MENU – RAT-FACE
EEK
A?
OW... WELL... SUIT Y'SELF – 'COURSE IT COULD PROVE DEAD UN'EALTHY – KNOW WOT I MEAN?
DISEASE, SQUIRE – PLAGUE EVEN
I MEAN – US RATS IS DIABOLICALLY UN'YGIENIC
AN' WE GOT DISGUSTIN' 'ABITS
AN' SMELL, COR – I'M UNBELIEVABLE I AM – 'AVEN'T 'AD A BATH SINCE THAT DIP IN THE SEWAGE AN' – 'ERE – I WISHT YOU WOULDN' KEEP WALKIN' AWAY WHILE I'M TALKIN' TO YOU...

HULLO BOOT OLD CHAPS – ANY NEWS FOR THE NEWSHOUND?
OH – HULLO B.H. (CALCUTTA) Failed
HOW ABOUT A STORY OF ONE PERSON'S COURAGEOUS STRUGGLE 'GAINST HARDSHIP AND DEPRIVATION?
– A MEMBER OF THE NOBILITY, ONE USED TO THE SIGHT OF THE GROANING BANQUET TABLE – ROAMING THE STREETS GIPPED BY THE PANGS OF HUNGER
GOODNESS GRACIOUSNESS – 'TIS A TALE TO WRING THE WITHERS
WHO ARE BEING THIS UNFORTUNATE PERSONAGE?
DAMMIT B.H. – I SHOULD HAVE THOUGHT IT OBVIOUS
I HAVEN'T HAD A BITE OF BREAKFAST
Q.274

I'M NOT AT ALL CERTAINING IF YOUR NOT HAVING HAD BREAKFAST CONSTITUTES A NEWS STORY, BOOT
HOWEVER —I'LL MAKE A FEW NOTES
ON MY NOTE-PAD
LET ME SEE... NAME ? BOOT *MMM* OCCUPATION ? DOG *MMM*
OF COURSE—WE MIGHT GET IT ON THE COOKERY PAGE
Q.275
—COULD YOU DESCRIBE WHAT KIND OF BREAKFAST IT WAS YOU DIDN'T HAVE

Q.276
NOW THEN, BOOT, THIS BREAKFAST YOU DIDN'T HAVE
I TAKE IT YOU DIDN'T HAVE CHAMPAGNE
I CERTAINLY DID ***NOT***
WITH CAVIARE... FOLLOWED BY KEDGEREE... DEVILLED KIDNEYS ...MIXED GRILL...
YOU ADMIT TO NOT HAVING HAD ALL OF THOSE...
'PON MY SOUL I DO
MMM MM MM MMMM... MY WORDS — THIS STORY ARE BUILDING UP NICELY
...THOUGH RAGING HUNGER ROAMS THE STREET BLASÉ SOCIALITE PASSES UP SUMPTUOUS CHAMPAGNE BREAKFASTS CONSISTING OF...

Q.277
DAMME, B.H., WHAT D'YOU MEAN BY CALLING ME A BLASE SOCIALITE ?
HAVING A CARE, SIR — DO NOT INTERFERING WITH THE FREEDOM OF THE PROD
I MEAN PRESS
PERHAPS YOU'D LIKE A VISIT FROM THE N.U.G. ? (THE UNION FOR JOURNALISTS WHO CAN'T SPELL)
HOW D'YOU FANCY BEING BLACKLISTED, BLACKLEGGED, BLACKBALLED ?
THE N.U.G. WOULD RESORT TO THAT ?
YES
WE'RE A VERY POOR UNION
WE DO A BIT OF PAINTING AND DECORATING ON THE SIDE

DAMME B.H.— YOU'LL NOT BROW-BEAT ME WITH YOUR TALK OF THE N.U.G.
NOTHING WILL STOP THIS FEARLESS REPORTER FROM FILING HIS STORY
HOLD THE FRONT PAGE !
— AND WHO WOULD WANT TO READ YOUR NONSENSICAL TARRADIDDLE OF MY NOT HAVING HAD BREAKFAST ?
NONSENSICAL TARRADIDDLING ? THIS ARE BEING A STORY OF GREAT SOCIAL SIGNIFICANCE
YOU ADMITTED TO NOT HAVING A CHAMPAGNE BREAKFAST ?
WELL — SINCE YOU'D PUT IT TO ME IN THOSE TERMS, I DID
OTHER PEOPLE HAVE TO MANAGE ON DOING WITHOUT A PIECE-OF-TOAST-AND-MARMALADE BREAKFAST
Q278

DAMME B.H., ALL I SAID WAS I HADN'T HAD BREAKFAST
IT'S NO USE WEASELING AND WHINING BOOT, THE STORY STAYS
YOU ADDED ALL THE CHAMPAGNE-AND-CAVIARE NONSENSE
WE INTEND TO STUN OUR READERS WITH THIS TALE OF BLATANT POWER AND PRIVILEGE
AND THERE'S A SPECIAL OFFER ON LOO-ROLLS THIS WEEK, TOO
Q.279
BY THE LORD HARRY, YOU SCURRILOUS SCRIBBLER— I'VE A MIND TO...
OH I'M KNOWING WHAT'S COMING NEXT— I'VE HEARD IT ALL BEFORE
— YOU'RE GOING TO OFFER A BRIBE — PAY ME TO SPIKE THE STORY
I CERTAINLY AM NOT
OH ?
IT DOESN'T COST ALL THAT MUCH YOU KNOW

BY THE LORD HARRY — DO I HEAR ARIGHT ?
ARE MY SENSES DECEIVING ME ?
IF YOU ARE WANTING A MEDICAL EXAMINATION I CAN GET IT FOR YOU WHOLESALE
ARE YOU TELLING ME YOU'LL ACCEPT MONEY TO NOT PRINT A STORY
ACCEPT MONEY ? THE VERY IDEA SURPRISES AND ASTONISHES ME
— I USUALLY HAVE TO TAKE LUNCHEON VOUCHERS
Q.280

YOUR STORY ABOUT THE BREAKFAST I NEVER HAD IS ABOUT TO BECOME A DEAD DUCK
OR AT LEAST A DEAD PORK PIE OR TWO
YOU ARE SPEAKING IN CONUNDRUMMINGS – WHAT...
CRASH
– I'M SPEAKING OF THE BUTCHER'S BOY – FOOLISHLY STRAYING FROM HIS CUSTOMARY ROUTE
TEAR UP THE FRONT PAGE!
GOODNESS GRACIOUSNESS – EYEWITNESS EXCLUSIVE...
IN FIGHT AGAINST BEEF-BARONS' UNJUST MONOPOLY
BRILLIANT MANŒUVRE BY RESOURCEFUL DOG...
MERCIFUL LIBERATION OF VAST QUANTITIES OF CHOICE COMESTIBLES
Q.281
...WHICH THE CALLOUS AND UNSCRUPULOUS ASSAILANT SCOFFED IN ITS ENTIRETY ALL BY HIS FLAMING SELF

Q.282
BOOT – I'VE MANAGED TO GET A FEW SUPPLIES IN
ZZZ
WITH A SPECIAL TREAT FOR YOU – SAUSAGES! A POUND OF BEN'S BEST
– WORKED LIKE A SLAVE I DID – RAN ERRANDS – DUG GARDENS – WASHED CARS
COR – THESE SAUSAGES DO LOOK SMASHIN'
BURP
AS PLUMP AN' MEATY AS OLE CYRIL SMITH – A POEM IN PORK
BOOT?
SAUSAGES BOOT
ARE YOU LISTENIN'?
YAWN
WELL ONE WAY OR ANOTHER YOU'RE GOIN' TO HAVE THESE SAUSAGES

Q.283
ONE DAY YOU'RE SCOFFIN' EVERY LAST SAUSAGE I OWN
THEN — WHEN I GET SOME SPECIALLY FOR YOU — YOU GO ALL ALOOF
WELL I CAN'T STAND IT
I BOUGHT 'EM SO YOU'RE GOIN' TO ENJOY 'EM
I SAID ENJOY 'EM — BUT THERE'S NO NEED TO BE RIDICULOUS

TAKE THAT SILLY GRIN OFF YOUR FACE AN' GIVE ME BACK MY FRYIN' PAN
GIVE IT BACK, BOOT-GIVE IT BACK I SAY
THIS IS AN EMERGENCY!
IT'S STUCK IT REALLY IS STUCK!
WELL IT STARTED OFF AS A PERFECTLY RESPECTABLE EMERGENCY
Q.284
WITH YOUR HELP IT'S DEGENERATING INTO A VULGAR LITTLE KNOCKABOUT ROUTINE

IT'S NO USE, BOOT, THIS FRYIN' PAN'S STUCK FAST
WAIT— I'VE GOT A NIDEA
I *THINK* THIS ROPE'S LONG ENOUGH
RIGHT— BRACE Y'SELF— ANY MINUTE NOW
— LET'S JUS' HOPE HE DRIVES PAST THE VET'S
Q.285

CRUMBS — LOOK, MAISIE
WHAT...?
TURN ROUN' MARLON — PAY NO ATTENTION
— HE'S JUS' LOOKIN' FOR AN EXCUSE TO TELL US ONE OF HIS LONG AN' 'STREMELY UNLIKELY STORIES
Q.286

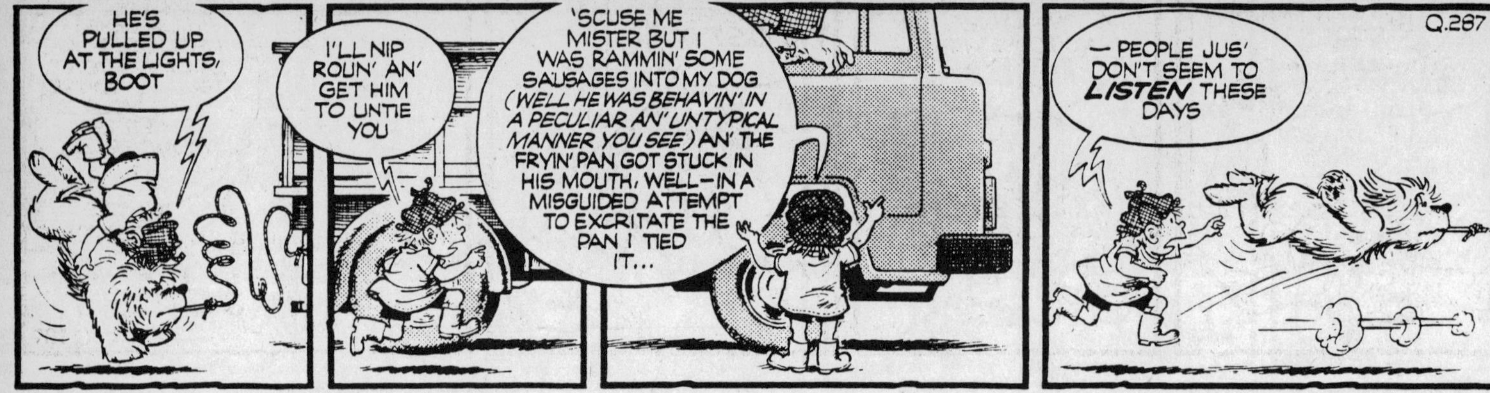
HE'S PULLED UP AT THE LIGHTS, BOOT
I'LL NIP ROUN' AN' GET HIM TO UNTIE YOU
'SCUSE ME MISTER BUT I WAS RAMMIN' SOME SAUSAGES INTO MY DOG (WELL HE WAS BEHAVIN' IN A PECULIAR AN' UNTYPICAL MANNER YOU SEE) AN' THE FRYIN' PAN GOT STUCK IN HIS MOUTH, WELL—IN A MISGUIDED ATTEMPT TO EXCRITATE THE PAN I TIED IT...
Q.287
—PEOPLE JUS' DON'T SEEM TO LISTEN THESE DAYS

BOOT, BOOT, DON'T WORRY BOOT —I'LL THINK OF SOMETHIN'
THWOCK
BOOT, BOOT—ARE YOU ALL RIGHT ? CRUMBS BOOT
Q.288
—WHERE'S THE FRYIN' PAN ?

WHERE'S THE FRYIN' PAN, BOOT ?
WHAT'VE YOU DONE WITH THE FRYIN' PAN ?
— YOU'VE *LOST* IT
— BUT NOT YOUR SENSE OF HUMOUR, A, BOOT, A ? DON'T TELL ME YOU'VE LOST YOUR SENSE OF *HUMOUR* .... A ?
Q.289

HERE HE COMES NOW, MARLON
PRETEND NOTHING HAPPENED
WE DON'T WANT ONE OF HIS LONG PECULIAR STORIES
WHAT-EVER YOU DO — DON'T ASK...
...HIM
WELLIN'TON — WOT 'APPENED — WHY WERE YOU AN' BOOT BEIN' TOWED IN THE AIR BEHIN' THAT LORRY AN'...
OH DON'T ASK ME — DON'T *ASK*
WELL NOW — *THERE'S* A BLESSED RELIEF
HOWEVER — SINCE YOU *DID* ...
Q.290

MY MUM SAYS THINGS'LL BE VERY SHORT THIS CHRIS'MAS
SO DOES MINE
MY MUM SAYS THINGS WON'T STRETCH AN' MONEY'S TIGHT AN' WHAT WITH ONE THING AN' ANOTHER ...
SO DOES MINE
CRUMBS
SIGH
—'MEMBER THE OLD DAYS ?
Q.291

you know maisie — something's worrying me about the whole father christmas business
REALLY BABY GRUMPLIN'?
well — i saw him outside the co-op hall
SO YOU DID, BABY GRUMPLIN'
and then — there he was in the street-market
ER... YES...THAT'S TRUE
— and smithson's and blower's and coming out of the crown — all those places one after the other
ER MMMM YES
Q.292
how can such an old man be so fit? he's never even out of breath
I'VE NEVER THOUGHT OF THAT, BABY GRUMPLIN'

WELL — I KNOW ALL OUR MUMS HAVE BEEN TELLIN' US CHRIS'MAS IS GOIN' TO BE A BIT TIGHT, AN' ALL
RHUBARB
RHUBARB
RHUBARB
RHUBARB
Q.293
— BUT I HAVEN'T BEEN PAYIN' ALL THAT MUCH ATTENTION
RHUBARB
RHUBARB
— NOT UNTIL YESTERDAY
WHEN I GOT THE SHOCK OF MY LIFE
RHUBARB
MADE ME FEEL QUITE SICK
— I SAW FATHER CHRISTMAS COMIN' OUT OF THE ***JOB CENTRE***
OH — NO-O-O-O-O

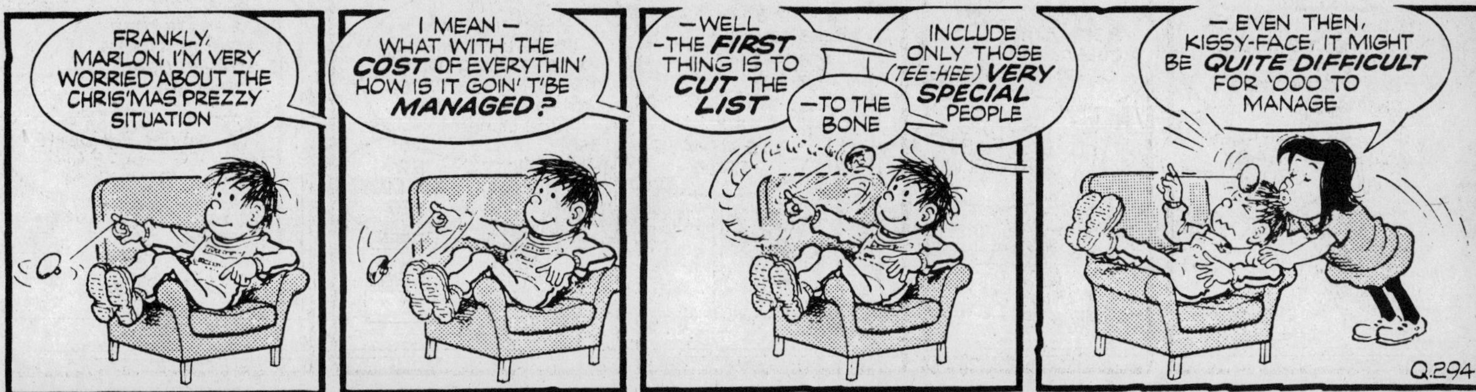

FRANKLY, MARLON, I'M VERY WORRIED ABOUT THE CHRIS'MAS PREZZY SITUATION
I MEAN — WHAT WITH THE ***COST*** OF EVERYTHIN' HOW IS IT GOIN' T'BE ***MANAGED?***
— WELL — THE ***FIRST*** THING IS TO ***CUT*** THE ***LIST***
— TO THE BONE
INCLUDE ONLY THOSE (TEE-HEE) ***VERY SPECIAL*** PEOPLE
— EVEN THEN, KISSY-FACE, IT MIGHT BE ***QUITE DIFFICULT*** FOR 'OOO TO MANAGE
Q.294

Q.295
MAISIE!
MAISIE?
YOU'RE NOT ROOTING ABOUT IN THERE LOOKING FOR PRESENTS ARE YOU ?
NO MUM
— I JUS' TRIPPED AN' FELL INTO THIS DRAWER

HUL-LO MAY LOVELY HANDSOME GENEROUS PREZZY-GIVIN' MAWLON —WHAT'RE YOU…
OH CRUMBS —YOU'RE NOT INVENTIN' THINGS AGAIN ARE YOU ?
Q.296
WELL— MAISIE — SINCE YOU SEEM SO KEEN ON GETTIN' A PREZZY I'M GOIN' TO 'AVE TO MAKE YOU ONE
OH— REELY ? OH JOY— MAKE ME ONE SUCH AS WHAT ?
W-E-L-L — HOW ABOUT YOUR VERY OWN DISCO WITH STEREO-SCOPIC LIGHTS AN' STROBOSCOPIC SOUND ?
— OR HOW ABOUT YOUR VERY OWN FOLD-UP LUXURY LINER WIV…
MARLON — BE PRACTICAL — FOR GOODNESS SAKE BE PRACTICAL
OK THEN — HOW ABOUT A BOOKMARK ?
THERE'S NO NEED TO BE THAT PRACTICAL

Q.297
MAISIE — YOU'RE NOT STILL ROOTING ABOUT FOR HIDDEN CHRISTMAS PRESENTS ARE YOU ?
— I'VE *TOLD* YOU THERE *AREN'T* ANY
MAISIE ?
WHY DON'T YOU ANSWER ME, MAISIE ?
MUM ?— HELP, MUM— I'M LOST !

Q.298
I'M GETTIN' VERY WORRIED ABOUT THE STATE OF THINGS IN GENERAL
—MARLON SAYS HE CAN'T AFFORD TO GIVE ME A PREZZY— AN' I'M BEGINNIN' TO BELIEVE HE MEANS IT
CRUMBS MAISIE —THE WHOLE WORL'S GOIN' TO RACK AN' ROONEY AN' ALL *YOU* C'N THINK OF IS MARLON GIVIN' YOU A PREZZY
WHY DON'T YOU STOP THINKIN' ABOUT MARLON GIVIN' YOU A PREZZY
WHY NOT THINK OF *SOMEONE ELSE* FOR A CHANGE
THINK OF SOMEONE ELSE ?
OH... WELLIN'TON...
Y'MEAN — *YOU'RE* GOIN' TO GIVE ME A PREZZY INSTEAD ?

OOH YOU'RE GORGEOUS YOU ARE WELLIN'TON —I DIN'T KNOW YOU CARED AN'...
GETTOFF MAISIE — I'M NOT GOIN' TO BUY YOU A PREZZY— I'M AS SKINT AS A NAKED NANA
—BUT I SAID MARLON WASN' GOIN' TO BUY ME A PREZZY AN' YOU SAID THINK OF SOMEBODY ELSE FOR A CHANGE SO I THOUGHT...
I MEANT —THINK OF SOMEBODY MORE UNFORTUNATE THAN YOURSELF — SOMEBODY WHO'S REALLY POOR SOMEBODY WHO'S GOT NOTHIN'
OH, I SEE
I SHOULD THINK SO TOO
Q.299
BUT IF THEY'RE IN THAT STATE I COULDN' POSSIBLY ASK THEM FOR A PREZZY

WHAT'S WRONG WITH YOU WELLINTON ? WHAT ABOUT SHOWIN' MAISIE SOME OF THAT WELL-PUBLICISED GOOD-WILL ?
LISTEN MAISIE —ALL YOU'VE DONE FOR THE PAST FORTNIGHT IS GO ON AN' ON ABOUT WHAT PREZZIES YOU MIGHT BE GETTIN'
—YOU NEVER THINK OF OTHER PEOPLE'S PROBLEMS NEVER EVEN CONSIDER OTHER PEOPLE'S FEELIN'S
OH, IS THAT SO ?
Q.300
I'LL BET NOBODY ELSE HAS BEEN KIND ENOUGH TO BUY DIRTY McSQUIRTY AN AIRWICK FOR CHRISTMAS

i don't know why they keep propagating the ridiculous story of Santa coming down the chimney
they must think we're somewhat lacking in intelligence — constantly reiterating such an obvious fabrication
well i'm on to it i can tell you — they can't deceive me any more
— i reckon mum lets him in through the back door
Q.301

I **KNOW** THEY'VE HIDDEN PREZZIES **SOME-WHERE** BABY GRUMPLIN'
Q.302
I MEAN — THEY **MUST'VE** MUSN' THEY ?
—THEY **ALWAYS** SAY THERE'S NOTHIN' — BUT THERE ALWAYS **IS**
NOTHIN'
I'VE LOOKED EVERYWHERE —THERE'S **NOTHIN'**
THEY WERE TELLIN' THE **TRUTH**
—IT'S ROTTEN WHEN A GIRL CAN'T TRUST HER OWN PARENTS

HEY, MAISIE Y'COMIN' OUT TO PLAY ?
I CAN'T —I'M NOT ALLOWED OUT
WOT'VE YOU DONE ?
WELL IF YOU MUS' KNOW —IT'S JUS' COS I WAS LOOKIN' FOR HIDDEN PREZZIES
— IT'S NOT FAIR — THEY SAID I WAS NAUGHTY AN' GREEDY AN' ALL STUFF LIKE THAT
WHADDAYA MEAN—WHEN DID THEY FIND THAT OUT ?
Q.303

Q.304
—WELL WHAT DID HE BRING US LAS'CHRIS'MAS BOOT ? NOTHIN'
AN' SIMILAR THE CHRIS'MAS BEFORE AN' THE CHRIS'MAS BEFORE THAT
— SO HE'S HARDLY LIKELY TO COME DOWN OUR CHIMNEY THIS YEAR —IS HE ?
—AN' EVEN IF HE DOES — WELL, ONE THING'S CERTAIN
— WE'LL BE AMONG THE FIRST TO KNOW

– a scarcity of prezzies owing to industrial action in Santa's work-shop, new baby
– that's what they told me
bloop
– the toys claimed they were being exploited – the gnomes came out in sympathy...
glop
... the reindeer came out for 'snow-money' and Santa came out in spots
blah
a likely tale
if you ask me they blew the money on that party they had last week
berk
Q.305

WHAT DID *YOU* GET FOR CHRIS'MAS WELLIN'TON ?
I GOT A DOLLY AN' A PAINTIN' BY NUMBERS AN'...
I GOT WHAT I GOT LAS' CHRIS'MAS AN' THE CHRIS'MAS BEFORE – *NOTHIN'*
Q.306
OH
WELL – IT'S NO USE FEELIN' SORRY FOR YOURSELF
AT *LEAST* – YOU HAVEN'T GOT THE *RESPONSIBILITY*

VROOM – VROOM VAROOM
VROOM – VROOM VROOM
IT'S MY NEW MACH II COTTON-REEL, MARLON
WOT'VE YOU GOT THERE, WELLIN'TON ?
VROOM- VROOM
DOES IT GO ?
GO ? JUS' LOOK AT THIS VROOM- OOM OOM-OOM
COR – I WISHT I 'AD ONE O'THEM
NO DOUBT YOU'D LIKE TO SWOP
Q.307
SWOP ? YOU MUS' THINK I'M STUPID
UNTIL THIS VERY MOMENT I WAS COUNTIN' ON IT

JINK- A-JINK- A-JINK
WHAT'S THAT WELLIN'TON ?
IT'S THE NEW JINKIN' COTTON-REEL, MAISIE
—IT'S GOIN' TO BE ALL THE RAGE
ALL THE RAGE ?
OH YES ANYONE WHO'S ANYONE WILL HAVE ONE OF THESE
JINK-A JINK
WOULD YOU SWOP FOR A PAINTIN' BOOK OR AN EEEK !
A-JINK- A- (GULP)
YET AGAIN, BOOT, I'VE BEEN SAVED FROM MYSELF
AN' WHOEVER'S DOIN' IT — I WISH THEY WOULDN'T BOTHER
Q.308

NEW YEAR RESOLUTIONS, BOOT
SOME PEOPLE THINK IT A SILLY IDEA
BUT I'M THE OLE-FASHIONED SORT
PEOPLE ARE FAR TOO SELF-SATISFIED
THERE'S NOTHIN' WRONG WITH TAKIN' A LONG HARD LOOK AT Y'SELF
— RUNNIN' A QUICK SPANNER ROUN' THE OLE CONSCIENCE
Q.309
— I'M DOIN' YOURS FIRST

RIGHT, BOOT, I'VE COMPLETED MY LIST OF YOUR NEW YEAR RESOLUTIONS
IT SAYS — "I, BOOT, RESOLVE TO BE A GREAT DEAL MORE OBEDIENT AN' LISTEN TO WHAT WELLIN'TON SAYS...
AN' TO STOP BEIN' A ROTTEN NUISANCE AN' BE A LOT MORE HELPFUL AROUN' THE HOUSE
AN' EAT AN' SLEEP A LOT LESS..."
R.1
— I HADN'T FINISHED

I HADN'T FINISHED READIN' THIS LIST OF NEW YEAR RESOLUTIONS ***I'VE*** MADE FOR ***YOU***
IT CONTINUES... "I PROMISE TO BE UNFAILINGLY GOOD-HUMOURED
— GOOD TEMPERED
— NO MATTER ***WHAT*** THE CIRCUMSTANCES"
R 2
— ARE YOU LISTENIN' ?

I AM NOW COMIN' TO THE ***MOST IMPORTANT*** PART OF THE NEW YEAR RESOLUTIONS I WROTE FOR ***YOU***
IT SAYS "IN ***NO CIRCUMSTANCES*** WHATEVER WILL I EVER SIT ON WELLIN'TON"
AN' IT SAYS IT IN ***BIG BLACK LETTERIN'***— IN ***ITALIC*** AN' ***UNDERLINED***
ON THE ***EXTRA-LARGE*** SHEET OF PAPER WHICH FOLLOWS THIS ONE
R 3
WHICH I AM GOIN' TO WRITE AS SOON AS CIRCUMSTANCES WILL ALLOW

WE COME NOW TO THE IMPORTANTANTEST PART OF THE MOST IMPORTANT PART OF THE RESOLUTIONS I WROTE FOR YOU
IT SAYS ... "I, BOOT, FULLY REALISE THAT CONTINUED SITTIN' ON WELLIN'TON CAN ONLY LEAD TO STARVATION AN' OTHER ADVERSE CONDITIONS
– ON ACCOUNT OF I, BOOT, CANNOT UNDO THE LARDER DOOR AN' BALANCE ON A CHAIR ...
AN' REACH THE PLATE OF COLD SAUSAGES WHICH LURKETH ON THE TOPMOST SHELF BEHIND ..."
R4
WHO'D IMAGINE SUCH EVIL GENIUS COULD LURK IN ONE SO YOUNG

HEY, BOOT, JUST A MINUTE – WE HAVEN'T FINISHED
THERE'S STILL THIS LIST OF RESOLUTIONS WHICH I WANT YOU TO STUDY AN' DIGEST
GLOP
R.5
A BIT MORE TIME ON THE STUDY ASPECT WAS MORE WHAT I HAD IN MIND

WELL— I'VE MADE A LIST OF MY NEW YEAR RESOLUTIONS NOW, BOOT
R.6
AN' I'M NOT DEALIN' IN TRIVIALITIES I C'N TELL YOU
THIS IS HARD TOUGH STUFF
THE SORT MANY PEOPLE LACK THE SELF-DISCIPLINE TO EVEN THINK ABOUT
AN' YET I KNOW I C'N CARRY IT THROUGH
I HEREBY RESOLVE TO NOT DRINK, SMOKE OR GAMBLE...

ANOTHER THING I'VE RESOLVED, BOOT, IS TO HELP OLE LADIES
YOU KNOW—WITH THEIR BAGS AN' STUFF
I'LL BET I'LL BE THE BEST OLE LADY HELPER FOR MILES AROUN'
R.7
WELL— THAT'S ONE RESOLUTION GONE BANG ALREADY
WHAT A DAY
YOU'D BE SURPRISED HOW WIRY SOME O'THEM OLE LADIES ARE
AN' TALK ABOUT SUSPICIOUS

WELLIN'TON — WHAT'S ALL THIS RUBBISH ABOUT YOU GIVIN' UP SMOKIN' ?
YOU DON'T SMOKE ANYWAY— WHY DON'T YOU DO SOMETHIN' DIFFICULT LIKE GIVIN' UP SWEETS
I HAVEN'T ANY SWEETS TO GIVE UP — THAT'S WHY MAISIE
JUS' COS I'M POOR THE OPPORTUNITY FOR STIMULATIN' SELF-DENIAL IS DENIED ME
NOW, IF SOME CONCERNED CITIZEN WERE TO OFFER ME A SWEET I COULD REFUSE IT
R.8
OH
WELL
GASP
VERY WELL THEN
WOULD YOU LIKE TO (MOAN) REFUSE ONE OF THESE ?
AAAAAAGH!
I'D BETTER STICK TO (SLURP GOBBLE) GIVIN' UP SMOKIN'

WELLIN'TON TOOK A SWEET
IN FAC' HE TOOK SEVERAL
AAAAA
'ULLO WELLIN'TON —WOT...?
RUN MARLON— EVERYBODY RUN!
AAAAAAAGH
—RUN —BEFORE THE SHOCK-WAVE HITS YOU
R.9

WHAT HAPPENED WHAT *HAPPENED*?
MAISIE OFFERED WELLIN'TON A SWEET AN' HE *TOOK* ONE
SEVERAL IN FAC'
HER ANGUISHED SCREAM WILL HIT US ANY MINUTE...
...NOW
AAAAAAAGH
THAT WAS AWFUL
TERRIFYIN'
I WANT MY MUM
MAYBE THEY'LL SET UP A FUND
IT'S NOT OVER YET— LISTEN
R.10
—THEY CALL HER THE *GLAZIERS' FRIEND*

CRUMBS, BOOT, MY NEW YEAR'S RESOLUTIONS'VE CAUSED ME NOTHIN' BUT TROUBLE
R.11
MAISIE HAD HYSTERICS — HALF THE WINDOWS IN THE DISTRICT GOT SHATTERED...
AN' ALL BECAUSE I MADE A RESOLUTION TO NOT START SMOKIN'
BOY — IF THE IMPERIAL TOBACCO COMPANY KNEW ABOUT *ME*....
LICK LICK

HE'S BEEN SITTING THERE FOR AGES— JUST **THINKING**
'TIS AN AWESOME PROCESS —REVEALING LITTLE OF ITS VIBRANT INTENSITY TO THE OUTSIDE WORLD
YET WITHIN THAT MIND A UNIVERSE TEEMS
PUZZLES ARE PONDERED
CONCLUSIONS REACHED
DECISIONS MADE
MAYHAP E'EN NOW BEGINS A COURSE OF ACTION WHICH WILL PLOT THE CHART FOR THE FUTURE OF THE WORLD
—STARTING WITH THE RISE AND FALL OF A PEANUT-BUTTER SANDWICH
R 12

HE SPENT **ALL** THAT **TIME**— **THINKING**—AND ALL HE THOUGHT OF WAS A PEANUT-BUTTER SANDWICH
SCOFF
MUNCH
GROFFLE
HOLD HARD THOUGH...
ALL HE THOUGHT OF WAS A PEANUT-BUTTER SANDWICH?
AT LEAST **HIS** THOUGHTS ACHIEVED FORM, **SUBSTANCE**
AND WHAT'S **WRONG** WITH A *(SLURP)* **HIGHLY DESIRABLE** PEANUT-BUTTER SAND-WICH?
OR AN **EVEN MORE** DESIRABLE **SAUSAGE** SANDWICH OR *(WHY DIVERSIFY)* A SAUSAGE **WITHOUT** THE SANDWICH OR **MANY** SAUS... WAIT... LET'S NOT OVERDO IT ON THE FIRST ATTEMPT
RIGHT THEN— BY THE LORD HARRY LET'S TO'T
THINK THINK THINK THINK THINK THINK THINK THINK THINK THINK THINK THINK
R.13
NO WONDER MANKIND RULES THE WORLD

WHEN YOUNG WELLINGTON THOUGHT — HE ENDED UP WITH A PEANUT-BUTTER SANDWICH
I THOUGHT, AND THOUGHT AND THOUGHT AND THOUGHT, AND WHAT DID I END UP WITH ? NOTHING
WAIT THOUGH — WHEN I THOUGHT — WHAT DID I THINK ?
THINK — THAT'S WHAT I THOUGHT
I SHOULD HAVE THOUGHT — SAUSAGES
INSTEAD OF WHICH — WHAT I THOUGHT WAS 'THINK-THINK-THINK-THINK-THINK'
MAYBE I'VE ENDED UP WITH A BOWLFUL OF PURE THINK
— I MEAN THOUGHT
R.14
LICK-LICK SCRATCH-SCRATCH RATTLE-RATTLE
I DON'T THINK I WAS CUT OUT TO BE AN INTELLECTUAL

MAYBE I CAN'T MANIFEST A SAUSAGE BECAUSE I'M NOT THINKING IN SPECIFICS
WHEN I THOUGHT, I JUST THOUGHT THINKS
I SHOULD HAVE THOUGHT SAUSAGE
NOW — IF I REALLY CONCENTRATE
SAUSAGE SAUSAGE SAUSAGE SAUSAGE
R.15
WELL COME ON WHAT DOES IT TAKE — THE BRAND NAME ?

R.16
HULLO BOOT OLD.... GOODNESS GRACIOUSNESS —ARE YOU IN PAIN ?
OH HULLO B.H. (CALCUTTA) Failed
AS A MATTER OF FACT I'M THINKING
DEUCED DIFFICULT BUSINESS I CAN TELL YOU
I'VE BEEN THINKING AND THINKING LIKE BILLY-O WITHOUT ACHIEVING ANY-THING WORTH-WHILE
HAVE YOU TRIED 'LATERAL THINKING', IT ARE SAID TO PRODUCE REMARKABLE RESULTS
LATERAL THINKING ?
OH— VERY WELL THEN
—BUT IF THIS IS ONE OF YOUR JOKES....

R.17
MMM
OOH
GRUNT
GROAN
OOGH AAGH—HEY, B.H. IS ANYTHING HAPPENING ?
A?
WHAT ?
HAPPENING ?
WHERE ?
HERE YOU FOOL— IS ANYTHING HAPPENING HERE ?
WELL— THERE ARE A LARGE HAIRY DOG LAYING ON HIS SIDE, GRUNTING AND GROANING LIKE BILLY'S HO AND...
GRUNTING ?
GROANING ?
I'M THINKING —THINKING OF SAUSAGES
OH....OF COURSE...DEARIE ME... I SHOULD'VE KNOWN THERE'D BE A RATIONAL EXPLANATION !

I HAPPEN TO BE EMITTING THE ODD GROAN BECAUSE OF THE INTENSITY OF MY *THINKING*
AND WHAT I'M INTENSELY THINKING IS *SAUSAGES*
IN THE HOPE MY THOUGHT WILL TAKE FORM AND A SAUSAGE WILL APPEAR BEFORE ME
AND I'M DOING IT IN *THIS* POSITION BECAUSE YOU YOURSELF RECOMMENDED *LATERAL THINKING*
AHA – *THAT'S* THE SPIRIT – *DOUBLE* LATERAL THINKING *WHAT?*
NOT REALLY – I SUDDENLY FELT DIZZY AND FELL OVER
R.18

WELL I'VE BEEN THINKING AND THINKING WITH PRECIOUS LITTLE TO SHOW FOR IT
WHO THOUGHT UP THIS 'LATERAL THINKING' TARRADIDDLE ANYWAY?
R.19
DOCTOR EDWARD DE-BONO
DE BONE-OH? WELL THE MONICKER SEEMS SOUND ENOUGH
WITH A NAME LIKE THAT YOU'D THINK HE'D HAVE MORE SENSE

WHAT LEADS YOU TO BELIEVE YOU CAN THINK A SAUSAGE INTO EXISTENCE
BECAUSE YOUNG WELLINGTON DID
EXCEPT THAT IT WAS A PEANUT BUTTER SANDWICH
LOOK— WHAT I'M SAYING IS HE SAT AROUND THINKING FOR AGES AND AGES AND ENDED UP WITH A PEANUT BUTTER SANDWICH
MAYBE IT ONLY WORKS FOR PEANUT BUTTER SANDWICHES
WELL I WOULDN'T SCORN ONE OF THOSE —LET'S TRY TO THINK ONE UP
PEANUT BUTTER SANDWICH PEANUT BUTTER SANDWICH PEANUT BUTTER SANDWICH
WITH A TOUCH OF MARMITE
R.20
DAMMIT, B.H., DON'T CONFUSE THE ISSUE

WELL WE WEREN'T ABLE TO MANIFEST EITHER A SAUSAGE OR A PEANUT BUTTER SANDWICH
MAYBE WE SHOULD HAVE BEEN EVEN MORE SPECIFIC
HOW D'YOU MEAN ?
STATE IN DETAIL EXACTEMENT WHAT KIND OF SAUSAGE WE'RE REQUIRING
AS LAID DOWN IN THE APPROPRIATE REGULATIONS
VERY WELL THEN— GIVE IT A GO
I AM CONCENTRATING ON A PORK SAUSAGE AS PER THE 'SAUSAGE AND OTHER MEAT REGULATIONS 1967'
...A MEAT CONTENT OF NOT LESS THAN 65% —80% OF THE 65% MUST BE PORK AND 50% OF THE 80% MUST BE 'LEAN MEAT' WHICH MAY CONSIST OF FAT, SKIN, RIND, GRISTLE...
STOP —CEASE— ABANDON THE PROJECT
LEAVE ME WITH SOME ILLUSIONS
IT'S LIKE HEARING THE WOMAN YOU MOST DESIRE DESCRIBED AS PER THE FAIR TRADING ACT
R.21

WHAT SARNIES'VE YOU GOT, MARLON?
I'VE INVENTED AN ACTION-PACKED FILLIN' OF MARMITE, PEANUT-BUTTER, 'NANA AN' PLUFFMAN'S PICKLE
JUST A MINUTE...
YOU HAVEN'T GOT THOSE GHARSELY SARNIES WITH AN INCH-THICK KETCHUP (YEUK) FILLIN' HAVE YOU?
NO
IT'S NOW 2½ CENTIMETRES THICK—I'VE GONE METRIC
R.22

THEM KETCHUP SANDWICHES ARE LETHAL, EVERY TIME YOU BITE ONE YOU SHOOT A GREAT STREAM OF STICKY KETCHUP ALL OVER...
R.23
WHAT'S TH'MATTER WELLIN'TON?
IT'S MARLON HERE WITH HIS ROTTEN KETCHUP SARNIES—HE'S A MENACE—A NABSOLUTE...
D'YOU MINE IF I GET ON WITH MY LUNCH
LOOK OUT—DUCK!
I DIN'T SEE NO DUCK
WOZZAT YOUR IDEA OF A JOKE?

 First published in Great Britain in 1984 by Mirror Books Ltd., Athene House, 66/73 Shoe Lane, London EC4P 4AB for Mirror Group Newspapers Ltd. Printed and bound in Great Britain by Spottiswoode Ballantyne Ltd., Colchester and London.

ISBN 0 85939 461 1